Sèvitè Voudou
Practical Voodoo Guide
Asamod ka

All rights reserved

No part of this book may be reproduced by any mechanical, photographic or electronic process, or in the form of a phonographic recording, without the prior written permission of the author.

According to article 12 of the Copyright and Related Rights Code, copyright is recognized independently of registration, deposit or any other formality.

Registration number at copyrighted.com: RIMepaRTatYYnhhp

If you republish, transform or reproduce this material, you may not distribute the modified material.

I made the cover by myself and I own the rights to the pictures I bought from Graphic River. License code: e05c8196-4b00-4474-a092-d8ccec8dc6aa

© 2024 ∴ Asamod ka

Index

Introduction .... 9 to 10
History of Voodoo .... 11 to 13
Syncretism .... 14 and 15
Pantheon of deities .... 17 to 20
Origin of the loas 21
Loas and their offerings 22
The priestly structure .... 24 and 25
Initiation .... 26 to 28
Constitution of the human being 29
Components of the soul .... 30 to 31
Reincarnation 31
The Rites and lineages (Nations) .... 33 to 36
The Colors and their uses .... 37 and 38
The Loas, colors and corresponding days 39
Moon Phases... 40
Types of requests and corresponding loas .... 40 and 41
The Altar .... 42 to 46
Offering to the ancestors .... 43 to 45
Utensils on the altar .... 45 and 46
Voodoo dolls 48
The possession .... 49 to 51
Rite of self-initiation 52
Recipes: oils, essences, voodoo powders .... 54 to 66
Potion to curse an enemy 59
Recipe for Papa Legba salt 61
Voodoo powders .... 62 to 65
Spells .... 67 to 92
Open paths or cut a curse 67
Lightning stone for protection .... 68 to 69
Getting rid of bad luck 70
Influence of dreams with gris gris 71
Voodoo binding with Erzulie Freda .... 71 and 73
Preparing a basic altar .... 73 and 74
Asking the loas for a favor .... 74 and 75
Voodoo curse .... 76 and 77
Simple voodoo spell to dominate someone 77
Voodoo spell to destroy an enemy 78
Remotely influencing someone .... 78 to 81
Voodoo doll – Spells .... 82 to 90
For burning desire 85

Doll to attract money 86
Revenge spell with the Djab ....87 and 88
Small sachet to curse someone 89
Mini coffin to cause death .... 89 and 90
Curiosities .... 91 and 92
Drawing the Veves .... 93 to 106
Veve of the Ghède spirits 94
Veve of Baron Samedi 95
Veve of Ogoun Ferraille ....96 and 97
Veve of Ogou Badagris 98
Veve of Aizan 99
Veve of Papa Legba .... 100 and 101
Veve of Erzulie Freda 102
Mamman Brigitte 103
Damballah 104
Veve of Carrefour 105
Glossary .... 108 to 116
Bibliography 117

Introduction

This book is my fifteenth published work, having already released titles on gypsy magic, chaos magic, quimbanda, santería, santa muerte, sumerian magic, vampire magic, and other esoteric systems. Twenty-five years of practice and study in the field of occultism have led me to investigate sources and compare them to ensure coherence and avoid contradictions.

I like my books to focus more on practical application, giving the reader tangible tools. This voodoo manual is not meant to be a guide to formal initiation into voodoo, a process that takes more than seven years of practice and in-person guidance from a hougan or mambo. However, it will enable the reader to develop a connection with the loa, set up their own altar, and perform a variety of rituals.

Additionally, I present in this manual practical rituals for those who wish to follow the path of the sorcerer or bokor, as well as detailed recipes for powerful powders and oils for ritualistic use.

Ninety percent of my readers enjoy doing practical and powerful spells to destroy adversaries, ward off rivals, attract sex and love, and open paths. This book follows that approach.

There exist various styles of voodoo, including the traditional and orthodox voodoo of Haiti, the more practical and informal Deka voodoo, the American hoodoo of Louisiana, the Gnostic voodoo, a more contemporary form, and various other styles.

This book focuses on Haitian Vodou in a less orthodox form, known as Deka Vodou. Haitian Vodou has a distinct tradition called the Deka system, which is characterized by a more flexible practice and a greater emphasis on the autonomy of the practitioner. It gives the sèvitè a less institutionalized approach, offering them the freedom to practice independently and adapt to their circumstances. Therefore, you can practice it wherever you wish.

Deka voodoo doesn't have strict rules like orthodox voodoo. In this system, the reader will have greater freedom to perform rituals according to their personal and spiritual understanding, without the need to always resort to priests (hougans) or priestesses (mambos) to mediate the relationship with the loas.

The rituals in Deka Vodou are more casual and individualized, with a greater emphasis on individual wants and desires, and a greater emphasis on interacting directly with the loas without relying on a hierarchical structure.

Why did I choose the title "Sèvitè Voudou"?

Sèvitè Voudou can be translated more directly as "voodoo practitioner" or "voodoo devotee", but without being properly initiated, so it is, dear reader.

A true Vodou experience requires years of practice and direct guidance from a Hougan or Mambo. You can't learn about Vodou just by reading a book. However, the reader is certainly capable of becoming a practitioner by establishing a connection with the loas.

History of Voodoo

Voodoo is a traditional African religion of great complexity, with strong animist elements. Syncretism with Catholicism emerged later in Haiti, during the colonial period.

This religious system can be written as "vodu" or "vodun," with "vodun" being the form used in the Fon language spoken in the Niger-Congo region. The Jeje-Fon people of Benin are where it got its start, with over 7 million followers.

The traditional name for this religious practice in West Africa is "Vodun," while the forms "vodou" or "voodoo" refer to variations developed in Haiti and New Orleans. Haitian Vodou is also known as "Sèvis Gine", or "Guinea Service".

West African tribes shared similar fundamental beliefs, which made it easier for neighboring ethnic groups to adapt their religions. These beliefs form the basis of Haitian Voodoo. The Fon religion, which is over 6,000 years old, had the biggest impact on the development of Voodoo.

Aside from the Fon tradition, also known as the Dahomey tradition, which persists in Africa, variants of this faith emerged in the Americas during the period of the transatlantic slave trade (16th to 19th centuries). Among these variations, notable ones include Candomblé in Brazil, Tambor de Mina in Maranho, Haitian Vodou, Santeria in Cuba, and Louisiana Vodou in the United States. However, Santería in Cuba is a distinct cult, with "La Regla de Arará" being the tradition that has its origins in Voodoo. "La Regla Arará" is an Afro-Cuban religious practice with roots in the religions of the Arará people of West Africa, an ethnic group that includes groups from what is now Benin and Togo.

Although it is often misunderstood and portrayed in a sensationalist manner, voodoo is a rich, fluid and syncretic spiritual practice that seeks connection with the divine and harmony with the natural and ancestral world.

Voodoo played a major role in Haiti's independence.

The slaves used voodoo as a form of resistance against the French colonists, under the leadership of the priest Dutty Boukman, who conducted the famous Bwa Kayiman ceremony in 1791.

During this ritual, a spiritual pact was sealed, invoking the loas to gain strength and start the Haitian Revolution, which began the fight for Haitian independence.

Still on the subject of syncretism, voodoo also included some Masonic symbols into the vevés (like the square and compass). At that time, there were several Masonic lodges in Haiti, and some loas were syncretized with Catholic saints and figures venerated by Freemasonry. For example, Ogou was associated with Saint James the Greater (Saint Jacques Majeur), a figure also relevant in the Masonic tradition. While Freemasons refer to God as the "Great Architect of the Universe" and the highest rank in Freemasonry is that of Grand Master, in voodoo, Bondyé (God) is referred to as "Grand Maître".

Freemasonry played a significant role during the Haitian Revolution. Some leaders of the Haitian Revolution, including Toussaint Louverture and Jean-Jacques Dessalines, were Freemasons.

Several Freemasons were also interested in participating in voodoo rites.

Haitian Voodoo

Haitian voodoo is one of the most widely recognized expressions of this religion. It is the result of a fusion of West African traditions, particularly those of the Fon and Yoruba peoples, with elements of Catholicism introduced by French colonizers. Practitioners of Haitian voodoo believe in a supreme God, Bondyè (Good God), who delegates his responsibilities to intermediary spirits called loas. Rituals involve chanting, dancing, sacrifices, and the incorporation of loas, who guide devotees in various aspects of life. These spirits are also known as "mysteries" or "saints."

It is believed that God, Le Gran Maître, is too exalted to care about worldly matters such as earthly life, but has left the loas as intermediaries between the divine and humans.

New Orleans Voodoo

Voodoo in New Orleans, Louisiana, developed in local Afro-descendant communities, resulting in a fusion of African, indigenous, and Christian practices. Although it shares similarities with Haitian Voodoo, such as belief in spirits and the use of ritual objects, it is distinguished by its syncretism with French and Spanish traditions, as well as the strong influence of legendary figures such as the famous voodoo queen Marie Laveau. In New Orleans, there is a strong focus on the use of amulets known as gris-gris and the practice of individual magic.

Voodoo in the Caribbean

Voodoo is also present in other Caribbean regions, such as Cuba and the Dominican Republic, where it mixes with other African-descendant religions, such as Santeria and Candomblé. These belief systems are similar to Voodoo, such as the worship of orishas and spirits. Each tradition has its own cultural and ritual differences.

Difference Between Voodoo and Hoodoo

It is important to distinguish voodoo from hoodoo, which is a magical practice based on African traditions, but without the religious structure of voodoo. Hoodoo is more focused on folk magic and witchcraft practices, often for purposes of protection, healing, or luck. Voodoo is a religion with ceremonies, priests, and an elaborate spiritual cosmology.

Sigils scratched, Veves.

Veves are important symbols in Haitian voodoo, similar to the scratched points in Kimbanda. Each vevê represents a specific loa and is drawn on the ground during ceremonies to invoke or honor those spirits. Created with materials such as flour, ash or dust, vevés function as portals that connect the spiritual world to the physical, facilitating communication and the presence of loas in rituals. For loas of the Rada line (white line), vevés are drawn with white corn flour. For loas of the Petro line (black line), they are typically drawn with charcoal or salt mixed with dark ash. Sometimes, a red powder made from chili peppers or powdered brick, or even red pemba, or even red pemba, is used.

Syncretism

Syncretism in Voodoo was due to the dominance of Catholicism during the colonial period when Haiti was a French colony. This process allowed Voodoo to survive and continue to be practiced, even under strong social and religious pressure. This process allowed Voodoo to adapt to the cultural environment without losing its spiritual essence. This strategy helped the Voodoo religion integrate into Christian societies, like Haiti and North America.

Within the context of slavery, where the practice of African religions was often prohibited or repressed, slaves found a way to preserve their spiritual traditions by associating the loas with Catholic saints. In this manner, they continued to venerate their traditional deities, hiding them under the iconography and names of Catholic saints.

Examples:

Bondyè, the supreme deity in Haitian voodoo, is commonly associated with the Christian God.

The loa Ogoun, the spirit of war and iron, was syncretized with Saint George, known for his connection with battle, or even with Saint James ("The Greater").

Erzulie Freda, the spirit of love, is associated with Our Lady of the Conception. Erzulie Dantor syncretized with "Our Lady of Mount Carmel" or "Virgin Mary".

Damballah is identified with Saint Peter or Saint Patrick.

Depending on the voodoo tradition or the sources, these syncretic associations may vary.

Voodoo in the USA

In the United States, particularly in New Orleans, voodoo underwent a syncretism with Catholicism as a result of the French and Spanish influence in the region. Over time, the religion evolved into what we know as New Orleans voodoo, incorporating elements of Christianity but keeping its African roots intact.

Voodoo gained great popularity through movies, especially for the depiction of dolls used to curse people and the creation of human zombies. However, the original purpose of the dolls was quite different — they served as symbolic replicas of patients and were used in healing rituals.

As for zombies, there is a more rational explanation: it is believed that they were people drugged with a powder containing hallucinogenic toxins, such as tetrodotoxin, extracted from fish such as fugu, which induced a state similar to death.

Voodoo can be used for both beneficial and harmful purposes, just like any spiritual tradition. As Kabbalah has a dark side and Umbanda has an equivalent in the left-hand path (Kimbanda), voodoo can also be applied to evil.

During the decline of colonial rule, Voodoo underwent an evolution that consolidated it as the national religion of Haiti, although Catholicism remained officially predominant. Voodoo became an essential symbol of the culture and unique identity of the rural Haitian population, reflecting their traditions and cultural traits.

Pantheon of Deities

In voodoo, particularly Haitian voodoo, deities are referred to as loas (or lwas). These spirits act as intermediaries between the supreme God and humanity, and are responsible for various areas of life. Although there is no strict and universally established hierarchy, some deities are considered more important or widely revered. Below is a basic hierarchy, organized by the most relevant deities:

Bondyè:

Bondyè is the supreme God and the creator of the universe, akin to the God of the Christian tradition. The name comes from "Bon Dieu" (good God). Bondyè is considered transcendent and distant, but it is not directly accessible to humans. For this reason, voodoo practitioners communicate with him through the loas, who act as spiritual intermediaries.

Papa Legba:

Legba is one of the most important loas in voodoo, playing the role of guardian of spiritual portals. He is the intermediary between humans and the spirit world, including other loas and Bondyè. Legba corresponds to the concept of Eshu in Kimbanda and to Elleguá or Legba of the Nagós. Without his permission, no other loa can be invoked, making him a central figure in all rituals. Legba also has a more aggressive and dark aspect, known as Legba Anti-Bon or Atibon.

Baron Samedi:

Baron Samedi is the loa of death, cemeteries and resurrection. He leads the ghede or guede (spirits of the dead) and holds power over life and death. Although his image is often associated with the dark side, Baron Samedi is also seen as a protective figure, preventing premature deaths and guiding souls on the path to the afterlife. His name is directly linked to 'Sabbath' ('samedi' in French), a day traditionally associated with rituals and cults of the dead in many cultures, including the Christian tradition, where Saturday is considered the Sabbath, a day of rest and spiritual reflection.

Erzulie (Ezili)

Erzulie is the loa of love, beauty, and fertility. There are different aspects of Erzulie, such as Erzulie Freda, who represents romantic love and sensuality, and Erzulie Dantor, who symbolizes protection and maternal love. Erzulie Freda, in particular, is associated with elegance and abundance, and is one of the most venerated loas. Erzulie Dantor is the wife of Ogoun Feray.

Ogoun

Ogoun is the loa of war, iron, technology, and politics, known for his strength and courage. He is often invoked during combat or to achieve success in endeavors that require power and leadership. Ogoun has several aspects or manifestations within his phalanx. One of these aspects is Ogou Feray, associated with military strength and war, and is summoned for protection in battle and to bring courage and determination. Another aspect is Ogou Badagris, who has a more aggressive nature and is linked to the destruction of enemies. Badagri (or Agbadarigi) is a city in Nigeria. Finally, Ogou Achade is a more diplomatic warrior, often invoked for negotiations and leadership.

Damballah

Damballah is the loa of wisdom and creation, symbolized by a serpent, representing purity, knowledge, fertility, and renewal. He is regarded as one of the oldest and most revered deities, associated with life, prosperity, and harmony. In the Rada ritual, Damballah is observed to reproduce through fission, manifesting as Damballah Wedo in his male form and Ayda Wedo in his female counterpart. In the Petro system, he assumes the form of Damballah Flambeau, an androgynous deity whose main attribute is omniscience.

Ayida Wedo

Ayida Wedo is the consort of Damballah and is associated with the rainbow, water, and fertility. Together, Damballah and Ayida Wedo represent continuity and cosmic harmony. Wedo was the name of the city of Ouhdeh, located in the region of the ancient Kingdom of Dahomey (present-day Benin).

Grand Bois:
A loa of nature, directly associated with forests, dense vegetation and the wild forces of the earth. The name "Grand Bois" means "Big Wood" in French.

Simbi

Simbi or Sim'bi is a Congolese loa of water, magic, and occult knowledge. He is often associated with mystical wisdom and communication, and is the protector of healers and spiritual practices linked to nature. In some Haitian traditions, he may also be invoked for negative spells. Occasionally, we can refer to loas in the plural because many loa names are actually phalanxes, governing hundreds of spirits that can manifest in their name. For example; Simbi Makaya is a great sorcerer, and served especially in the Sanpwel, secret societies. Simbi Anpaka is a loa of plants, leaves, and poisons.

Agwé

Agwe is the loa of the sea and everything related to navigation and aquatic life. He is invoked by fishermen and sailors, and is also responsible for protecting sea voyages.

Guède or Ghède

Guèdes are loas that are connected to the dead and the underworld. In addition to Baron Samedi, other loas, such as Guède Nibo, oversee the spirits of the deceased and are accountable for the transition between life and death. They are often portrayed in a festive and irreverent manner.

The ghède can be invoked for everything from spells against enemies to divination, and even for magic linked to eroticism.

Other Important Loas

Marasa: Twin loas associated with childhood and duality.

Mamman Brigitte: Wife of Baron Samedi, who is also linked to the dead and the cemetery, but with an origin strongly syncretized with the Saint Bridget of Christianity.

In the voodoo pantheon, there are deities that represent forces of nature, like the Orishas in Umbanda and Candomblé. For example:

Simbi, god of health and guardian of springs and seas. **Águé-taroyo**, the god of the sea, with fair skin and blue eyes, has dominion over everything related to the sea, including natural agents. **Mad Attiso**, called Docteur Feuilles (Doctor Leaves) is the protector of healers; a wise god, he knows all the healing properties of plants.
Other figures are: **Sobo**, god of lightning; **Bade**, god of the wind; **Agaú Tonne**, god of storms and thunder.

"Konnen lwa ou anvan ou fè rituèl yo."

(Know your loa before performing the rituals.)

Origin of the Loas:

In Haitian Vodou, the loas are diverse and include both spirits of human ancestors and supernatural entities of non-human origin.

Ancestral Spirits:

Ancestral Spirits: Some loas are associated with ancestors of specific families (zansèt yo) or communities. These are the spirits of people who have lived and died and whose souls now act as guides and protectors for the living. They may have been slaves or members of African communities before their death.

Supernatural Spirits: Other loas are considered spirits that were never human. These spirits have more mythological origins and are associated with aspects of nature, such as rivers, trees, or cosmic forces. They play specific roles and possess attributes that are not directly related to past human lives.

These are just a few main loas revered in voodoo, and their importance can vary depending on the region, spiritual lineage, and needs of the practitioners. Each loa possesses distinct characteristics and exhibits specific actions, resulting in a vast and rich cosmology.

The loas are represented in voodoo temples (hounfort) by the use of sequined and beaded flags (drapo sèvis). Most temples have at least two drapo sèvis: one that symbolizes the congregation (ounfo) and one that represents the loa they worship. These flags highlight the transcendent beauty of the loa and the strength and power of the active presence of the deities within the ounfo during rituals. For this reason, flags are considered some of the most sacred and valuable ritual implements.

Loas and their offerings

For your information, I am sharing some suggestions for offerings (including animals) to the loas. However, it is important to check whether it is illegal to kill animals for consumption in your country, city, or region. If this is the situation, it is possible to opt for more straightforward offerings, such as fruits, prepared meals, cigars, and alcoholic beverages.

Loa	Offerings
Agwé	Fish, seafood, shrimp, rum, silver coins, shells, coconut, white flowers. White and blue candles.
Azaka	Corn, bread, rice, beans, yam. Blue and red candles.
Baron Samedi	Black chicken, black goat, roasted peanuts, rum with peppers, cigars (lit), spicy meat, coins, sugar cane. Purple and black candles.
Danballa e Ayida-Wedo	Eggs (boiled), black chicken, rice, milk, roast pork, spring water, rice porridge, honey, white flowers. White candles.
Erzulie Dantor, e Erzulie Freda	White dove, rice, sweet cakes, roast pork, cigarillos, rum, knives, silver coins. Pink or light-blue candles.
Ghède spirits	Black rooster, black goat, coffee in a cup, spicy food, rum, cigars, cookies. Black and purple candles.
Maman Brigitte	Black chicken, rum with pepper, coffee in a cup, fine cigarillos, dark beer, white lilies. White and purple candles.
Ogoun	Red rice and beans, red rooster, mutton, rum, corn, lit cigars, metal knife. Red or white candles.
Papa Legba	Spotted rooster, roast chicken, smoked meat, rice, yam, rum, coffee in a cup, sugar cane. Red or white candles.

Basically all loas like rum, cigars should be offered lit (for female loas they are women's cigarillos). Coffee should not be offered in grain form, but rather liquid coffee.

Offerings can be placed on the altar or on a loa's "veve" drawn on the ground. In a later chapter, I will discuss "veves" more thoroughly.

22

The Priestly Structure:

Priests: Both of them have important roles as spiritual leaders and intermediaries between humans and the Loas. The highest ranks in the hierarchy are the papaloi (or papaloa), whose function is similar to that of a bishop, and the high priestess, the mamaloi (or mamaloa).

Important role: In voodoo, the hougan (priest) and mambo (priestess) are not just "spell casters"; they also act as spiritual healers for the community. They care for the mental and emotional health of practitioners, using rituals, herbs, and connection with the loas to balance body, mind, and spirit. These spiritual leaders guide and heal, addressing trauma, anxiety, and inner conflicts. They also provide a form of collective and individual therapy in harmony with ancestral and spiritual beliefs.

In addition to hougan and mambo, there are other roles and hierarchies associated with practitioners. Here are some of the key terms:

Hounsi: The initiates, both men and women, serve the loas. They are under the hougan or mambo in the hierarchy and assist in rituals, as well as being part of the choir. Hounsi has different levels, and they can get better with time and experience. After being initiated, the hounsi can take part in the rituals more actively, for example as a member of the choir of singers. The term "hounsi" means "husband" or "wife" of the loas.

Bokor: a practitioner of voodoo who has the ability to work with both "good" and "bad" magic. The bokor (or bocor) is often associated with more "practical" magic, such as the creation of amulets (gris gris), and may also be a hougan or mambo. The bokor has a wide range of skills; in addition to being a sorcerer, he is also a healer (docteur feuille), with a profound knowledge of the medicinal secrets of Haitian plants. However, he is often associated with objects or fetishes called ouanga (wanga), which are most often used to cause harm. Wanga is more than just a fetish or amulet, but a wide range of magical practices. It should be noted that the term "bokor" holds a somewhat negative connotation within Orthodox Voodoo, as it is commonly employed to denote the "sorcerers" of Makaya Voodoo.

Sèvitè: is a more general term that designates those who serve the loas. It may pertain to any practitioner of voodoo, irrespective of their hierarchical rank, including those who have not yet been initiated.

Kanzo: the initiation process in voodoo is known as "kanzo". During this process, individuals undergo various stages to attain the status of hounsis, hougan, or mambo. Kanzo is divided into three main levels:

Hounsi Kanzo: the lowest level of initiates, responsible for tasks like dancing and singing in rituals.

Sèvitè Kanzo: an intermediate level, involving more spiritual responsibilities.

Asògwe: the highest level of initiation, attained by a hougan or mambo. A hougan asògwe or mambo asògwe has the power to initiate others into voodoo.

Emperor or **La-Place:** the master of ceremonies during rituals, is responsible for organizing the space and ensuring that the rituals are performed correctly. He plays a crucial role alongside the hougan or mambo, initiating the ceremonies and greeting the loas.

Confiance: the temple administrator.

Kokò: the spiritual advisors or elders of the community who possess a vast knowledge of traditions and rituals, despite not being priests.

Initiation:

There are three levels of initiation in orthodox Vodou, which are achieved sequentially as the individual deepens his or her knowledge and tenure in the Vodou community. All degree levels of initiation are open to both men and women.

Vodouist or voodooist is a term used to describe a person who participates in ceremonies, gets advice and medicinal treatments from the hougan or mambo, and does activities related to voodoo.

An uninitiated person who is attached to a specific peristyle, regularly attends ceremonies, and appears to be being prepared for initiation is classified as a "hounsi bossale". The term "hounsi", originating from the Fon language of Dahomey, means "bride of the spirit", although in Haiti it is used for both men and women. Bossale means "wild" or "untamed", in the sense of a wild horse. In another context, "bossale" can also refer to loa spirits that are considered unwanted or troublesome.

First degree:

The first degree of initiation bestows the title of "hounsi kanzo." The word "kanzo" comes from the Fon language and means "fire", and the fire ceremony, also called Kanzo, gives its name to the entire initiatory cycle. Individuals who undergo the kanzo can be compared to those who have been baptized in the Christian tradition.

During a voodoo ceremony, the hounsi kanzo dress in white, form the choir, and are often the prime candidates to be possessed by the loa for the first time. The ritual can last up to a week. It includes a head washing, known as "laver tête." After the "laver tête" ceremony, sequined flags and "govis" vases are brought into the "djévo" room, veves are drawn on the floor, and doves and chickens are sacrificed. The initiates lie down on mats near the sign of their particular guardian spirit. At this point, each initiate is possessed by his or her guardian loa (Maît-tête, Head Master). Now the initiate, with the loa animating his or her body, is finally free to eat after the long fast, and often gorges himself or herself on the meat of the animal sacrifice.

Second degree:

The second degree of initiation is called "si puen," which comes from French "sur point," which means "at the point" or "on the point.". This term refers to the fact that the initiate undergoes specific ceremonies and is sponsored by a particular loa. From this point on, the individual is recognized as a hougan or mambo and gains the right to use the "asson", a sacred rattle that symbolizes his priesthood.

Individuals who attain the status of "si puen" may be compared to shepherds in Christian traditions. During ceremonies, they are responsible for leading prayers, chants, and rituals. They are often chosen for possession by the loas. Once initiated as "sur point," they have the power to perform both hounsi kanzo and "si puen" initiations.

Third degree:

The third and highest degree of initiation is the "asogwé". The "asogwe" houngans and mambos can be compared to bishops in Christian traditions, as they have the authority to consecrate new priests. Those who attain the "asogwe" degree can initiate others into the "kanzo", "si puen" and "asogwe" levels.

During a ceremony, the asogwé are the supreme authority in ritual proceedings, unless a loa manifests through possession, at which point the lwa assumes command. In addition, the asogwe is consulted as a last resort when the presence of a specific loa is required. An asogwe is said to "have the asson", referring to the power to confer the asson on another initiate, thus elevating the latter's rank to that of an asogwe.

Even a hougan or mambo asogwé must respect the authority of those who initiated him, as well as that of the asogwé who were initiated before him. Furthermore, he must defer to the opinion of the hougan or mambo who initiated his own initiator, and so on, maintaining a chain of respect and hierarchy that goes back to his predecessors.

Animal sacrifices

Although animal sacrifice may seem socially unacceptable, it is common for people to raise animals for food in the countryside. It is important to remember that Haiti is a large rural area where people raise animals for food. Therefore, the act of killing an animal for sustenance is normal for these people. Furthermore, poverty is high in Haiti, and not everyone has access to meat. Voodoo ceremonies are one of the few opportunities to eat cooked meat after the rituals.

Constitution of the human being

The concept of the human being (body, subtle bodies and soul) is a little complex, let's take it one step at a time:

In voodoo, the human being is considered to be composed of five parts:

Corps cadavre (physical body)

N'âme (vital energy, prana, chi)

Z'etoile (personal star, destiny)

Gros bon ange (spiritual soul)

Ti bon ange (soul, in the sense of charisma, personality)

Corps Cadavre refers to the perishable body. **N'âme** is the vital energy that allows the body to function during life, equivalent to the oriental chi. **Z'etoile** refers to the star of an individual's destiny, it is the future self towards which we all walk. **Gros bon ange** (literally "great good angel") and **Ti bon ange** ("little good angel") constitute, so to speak, the soul of the individual.

During gestation, the gros bon ange enters the human body and represents a portion of the universal energy, the state of consciousness that all humans possess. In contrast, ti bon ange is the individual soul or essence that develops throughout life, constituting each person's personality. It is this "little soul" that travels outside the body during dreams and also when the body is possessed by a loa.

The Human Soul itself

In the Haitian Vodou system, the complete soul is composed of several parts, each with specific functions. Here are the main components:

Components of the Soul:

Gros Bon Ange (or Great Good Angel):

Description: represents the pure and sacred spiritual essence of the individual. It serves as a spiritual guide and protector, maintaining a connection to the spiritual world.

Function: protects the soul and guides the person spiritually.

Petit Bon Ange (or Little Good Angel):

Description: represents the individual and personal part of the soul, which is more connected to daily experiences and the egoic self.

Function: relates to everyday life, emotions and personal behaviors.

Ti-Bon-Ange (or Little Good Angel):

Description: another aspect of the soul that is associated with personality and the innermost self.

Function: influences personal characteristics and the way a person interacts with the world.

Nanan-Bouclou:

Description: represents the part of the soul that is connected to ancestry and familiar spirits.

Function: maintains the connection with ancestors and family tradition.

Complete Soul Summary:

Gros Bon Ange: The spiritual and sacred essence, guide and protector.

Petit Bon Ange: The personal and emotional part of the soul, related to everyday life.

Ti-Bon-Ange: It influences the personality and the inner self.

Nanan-Bouclou: connects with ancestry and family spirits.

There is also a transcendental concept (external to the human soul) which is the individual's guiding star or destiny (Z'étoile), "The Star".

Reincarnation:

Voodoo suggests that the soul (Gros Bon Ange) can reincarnate into new bodies over time, but it is believed that the soul can only reincarnate up to 16 times. After these reincarnations, the soul is liberated and returns to the cosmos, merging with the primordial forces or the cosmic whole, losing its individuality. This cycle of reincarnations serves as a form of purification and spiritual learning, until the soul is finally reintegrated into the universe.

The Rites and Lineages (Nations)

Voodoo includes several rituals, not just one, as one might assume. Each rite was originally connected to a specific African community that was brought to Haiti. However, as the different ethnicities merged, the gods and rituals became syncretized.

The most prestigious rite in Haitian Vodou is the Rada or Arada, which originates from Dahomey. This style is that of Orthodox Vodou. The Nagó (Yoruba) and Ibó rites, originating from Guinea, ended up being almost completely integrated into the Rada rite. On the other hand, the Petro rite, of Congolese origin, remained more distinct, although it mixed with other rituals from Congo and Angola. This style is practiced in Makaya Vodou.

Positive Rada Rite / Orthodox Vodou:

Origin: Originating from Dahomey (present-day Benin), this rite is the oldest and most prestigious rite in Haitian voodoo. Its name derives from Arada, a Dahomey deity who originated in the Gulf of Guinea. Arada is also the name of a city in Guinea, which is considered to be a mythical land.

It focuses on benevolent and ancestral loas, which are connected to aspects of balance, harmony and good energy. Rada ceremonies tend to be quieter and more formal, with dances and music that emphasize serenity. Ritual offerings include offerings of food and drink, such as breads, fruits, and juices.

Examples of Rada loas: Damballah, Ayida Wedo, Papa Legba, Agwé, Erzulie.

Environment: Rada rituals are performed in temples, known as hounfort, or outdoors in spaces specially dedicated to different ceremonies, such as chapels dedicated to the deities. The element associated with these loas is water. This rite combines elements of Christianity and white magic.

A Rada ceremony can be held either in a temple known as a hounfort or outdoors. Saturday is the preferred day for celebrations, which can take place during the day or night. At the entrance of the temple, tables are set up with a variety of food, such as bread, fish, poultry, fruits, soft drinks, and sweets, so participants can take whatever they want.

The hounfort, also referred to as hounf, hounfor, or houmfor, is a shed that consists of distinct compartments known as peristyles, which are supported by columns. The central column through which the loas ascend and descend is called a poteau-mitan and is richly ornamented. It can be a cylindrical pillar made of cement or wood, in the center of the temple. Papa Legba is reputed to be the one who watches over this poteau-mitain pillar. The peristyle is decorated with the coat of arms of the republic and an effigy of the president. It is dedicated to different types of rituals. Vevés are drawn on the floor around the poteau-mitain.

Petro Rite (or Petwo) / Makaya Voodoo:

Origin: Originating from the Congo and Angola region.

Associated with more energetic and sometimes aggressive loas who can deal with more pressing and conflicting issues.

Petro rituals tend to be more intense and energetic, with dancing and chanting that evoke a more powerful and dynamic energy. The rhythms of Petro loas are played on tanbou fey drums, which are equipped with a rope rim that holds the leather stretched over the drumhead. The Petro rite may include elements of protection and defense, reflecting the more combative nature of the Petro loas.

Example of Petro loas: Baron Samedi, Baron Cimerere (Lord of the Cemetery), Ogoun, Guede, Brigitte, Carrefour, Marinette, Erzulie Dantor (said to have a dark side as well). Carrefour (or Kafou) is an important loa, associated with aspects of power and transformation, both materially and spiritually. The name "Carrefour" means "crossroads" or in French, reflecting the role of this entity in spiritual and physical intersections.

Environment: Rites also performed in hounforts, but with a more dynamic and vibrant atmosphere compared to the Rada. The element associated with these loas is fire. They are rough and violent loas, who can do both good and evil. The typical color of the Petro rite is red, an allusion to the fire and blood used in sacrifices.

The term "Petro" originates from a black hougan named Don Pedro, who immigrated to Santo Domingo in the 18th century. It is also related to the cult of the serpent "Dan", which was associated with the name "Petro".

In voodoo, the belief in dualism holds that the two polarities, namely good and evil, light and darkness, complement each other to maintain cosmic balance. Many loas have both a positive and a negative side, and one cannot exist without the other. For this reason, both the Rada and Petro loas are worshipped equally.

Orthodox Voodoo, also known as Traditional Voodoo or Rada Voodoo, maintains the oldest and most traditional practices of Voodoo, including rituals, ceremonies, and beliefs that have been preserved since colonial times.

Makaya Vodou, also called Petwo or Petro Vodou, is a more dynamic and pragmatic tradition, characterized by intense rituals and powerful energy. It adopts an assertive and active approach to magic and protection, invoking the most aggressive and intense loas of the Petro line.

Other Styles

Nagô Rite:

Origin: based on the Yoruba tradition of Nigeria.

It focuses on loas related to aspects of everyday life, with rituals that combine elements of protection and prosperity.

Ibó Rite (or Igbo):

Origin: Originating from the Abia region, Ibo tribe, in Nigeria.

Similar to the Nagó, but with specific variations in practices and deities worshipped.

Differences:

Nature of Loas: the loas in the Rada rite are generally more benevolent and associated with prosperity and balance, while the Petro loas are more energetic and can be invoked to deal with difficult or conflicting situations.

Ceremonial Environment: Rada tends to be more solemn and structured, while Petro is more dynamic and intense. Other rites, such as the Nagó and Ibó, bring influences and practices specific to their regions of origin.

These differences reflect the rich diversity within Haitian Vodou, where each rite contributes its own spiritual approach and ritualistic practice.

"Pawòl ou se yon kle; louvri pòt sèkèt yo."

(Your words are a key; they open the doors of secrets.)

The colors and their uses

The colors have mostly the same meaning as other traditional magic systems.

White: is used in spells for spiritual cleansing, removing omens, protection, blessing, healing, helping others, reverse spells, restoring health, and all things positive. White is associated with gentle, non-invasive energies.

Red: red represents love, passion, romance, energy, lust, fertility, attention, or sexuality. Red is associated with both strong and soft energies and can be coercive or subtly suggestive. The color red is often used for charms, love spells, sexual magic, and seduction. Red is also associated with the Petro loas and the element of fire.

Purple: workings using the color purple are typically for power, psychic ability, command, compulsion, controlling or binding others to your will. Spells of power, invocation, and control include the color purple. Purple can also be used for peace, protection, and abundance. It is associated with both strong and soft energies, and can be either coercive or subtly suggestive.

Green: green is associated with spells to attract money, wealth, and prosperity, and is used in spells for games of luck, fertility and business success. When one wishes to influence matters related to finances and abundance, uses green. Green is associated with energies that can be both intense and gentle, acting in a forceful or suggestive way.

Black: black can be used to remove evil or cause harm. Black, for example, is used to ward off negativity, protect, or remove negative people from your life. The color black can cause harm or destroy someone. Black is often associated with rituals of imposition, curses, tricks, coercive magic and summoning rebellious spirits.

Yellow: the yellow color is associated with mental agility, communication, quick action, and overall academic success. Yellow embodies gentle energies and has the ability to be coercive or subtly persuasive.

Pink: pink is used in works to attract love or success. Pink is associated with gentle energies.

Blue: for health, peace and abundance. Blue is associated with gentle energies and can be coercive or suggestive.

Brown: for practical and material blessings, legal proceedings, and neutrality. Brown is associated with strong or soft energies and can be coercive or suggestive.

Orange: for recognition, control and creativity. Orange is associated with strong or soft energies, and can be coercive or subtly suggestive.

Colors can also be associated with pins with a round head of a specific color.

Red pin: for power, sex, strong and dominating love.

Black Pin: to repel black magic, or to cause harm.

White pin: for magic in general, positive magic, healing.

Pink pin: for love, tranquility.

Green pin: for money, or health.

Blue pin: spirituality.

Yellow pin: material success, social success, intellect, self-esteem.

Purple: spirituality, protection.

The loas, colors and corresponding days

Loa	Day	Color
Agwé	Thursday	White and Blue
Ayida-Wedo	Monday or Tuesday	White and Blue
Azaka	Friday and Saturday	Blue and Red
Baron Samedi	Saturday	Black and Purple
Danballa	Thursday	White
Erzulie	Tuesday and Thursday	Pink, light-blue
Lasiren	Thursday	Blue-green
Ogoun	Monday, Friday, Saturday	Red
Papa Legba	Monday	Red and Black
Simbi	Tuesday, Thursday, Friday	White and Red

You can use one candle of each color, such as white or blue for Agwé, or a two-color candle, combining the two colors into a single bicolor candle.

Moon Phases

The rules are the same as any magical tradition...

Crescent Moon: ideal for attracting, increasing and manifesting intentions. It is a favorable phase for working on projects of growth, amplification, and fulfillment of desires.

Full moon: associated with the height of magic power and fulfillment. It is a powerful phase for love spells, abundance, and the fulfillment of great intentions. The energy of the Full Moon is intense and can be used to strengthen and enhance magical workings.

Waning Moon: used to diminish, cleanse and remove negative influences. It is a time to repel, reduce and deal with issues that need to be removed or diminished.

New moon: symbolizes renewal and new beginnings. It is the ideal time to set intentions, set new goals and focus on achieving new projects.

For love work, choose a Full Moon or a Waxing Moon. However, if you want to hurt a couple's relationship or drive away a lover, choose a Waning Moon.

The Waning Moon is the most appropriate phase for casting hate spells or preventing and repelling adversaries. In this phase, energy is decreasing, making it ideal for reducing, eliminating, or weakening negative influences and keeping unwanted people away.

Types of Requests and their corresponding Loas:

To open paths, improve communication, create new opportunities, and attract luck, Papa Legba is invoked. He acts as an intermediary between humans and the loas, facilitating communication and helping to resolve conflicts.

For ardent love, beauty, luxury, prosperity, and protection: Erzulie Freda.

For love that's more sentimental or maternal: Erzulie Dantor.

For strength, success, work, war against enemies, and material abundance: Ogoun.

To reap the rewards of hard work, success, and material wealth: Azaka Medeh.

For health, healing, protection from illness or death: Baron Samedi.

For wisdom, renewal, tranquility, spirituality, intuition: Damballa.

For vitality, fertility, spiritual protection, better self-esteem, and spirit: loas Ghéde.

All loas possess the ability to perform various magical works. For example, Baron Samedi can be invoked for powerful magic, scrying, necromancy, or revenge rituals. Additionally, all loas can be invoked for protection.

The Altar

You can build a wooden hut or a small room (such as a garage) in your home, as long as this room is away from your bedroom. It is not recommended to sleep or have sexual relations at the same place where voodoo spells and offerings are performed.

This division is a kind of "Kay Myste" (from the French caille des mystères, the house of secrets). These are small buildings, usually between 5 and 7 meters in size, where individual altars are built for each loa that the owner of the kay myste worships. These altars are made of common materials that can be found anywhere in the world and are known for their beauty and uniqueness. In Haiti, it is common for these altars to be built directly on the earthen floor.

Your kay myste can be in a small space in your bedroom or living room. In Haiti, it is generally believed that it is not good to sleep in the same place as objects consecrated to the loas, especially with a person of the opposite sex, unless sex is forbidden in any way. You can separate this area with a curtain or set aside an entire room for the service of the loa. The following instructions will help you build a basic altar of some sort for any specific loa.

Basic home altar:

It should be in a different room than your bedroom.

In Haiti, when a Vodou practitioner wishes to build an altar dedicated to a specific aspect of a loa, it is common to acquire religious objects that are associated with that loa. For an altar dedicated to a particular loa, use a cloth that is the color of the loa, for example, purple or black for Papa Legba.

Next, a Houngan or Mambo prepares and consecrates the altar. Some are set up directly on the earthen floor, while others are on platforms of planks or cement.

Take a white cloth and soak it in water with the first urination of the morning. You could also substitute vinegar for the urine. Let the cloth air dry, if possible. Cover your altar table with it, and subsequently lightly mist it with your preferred fragrance. If you can find four small stones near your home, clean them by soaking them in coarse salt and rinsing them well. A stone should be placed in each corner of your altar. Clean a wine bottle, glass bowl, or other vessel and then fill it with water. It is recommended to exclusively utilize glass or crystal instead of metal or earthenware. After blessing the water, place it in the center of your altar and stir in three parts anise liquor or white rum.

It is customary in Voodoo to baptize ritual objects by giving them a name. You can take a bunch of basil and anoint the baptism over your glass of water, which will be a powerful passage for spiritual energy. You can give it any name you wish.

In a glass candlestick, place some earth collected near your home and a few grains of coarse salt. Rub a white candle with a little vegetable oil from the middle to the top and then from the middle to the bottom. While oiling the candle, concentrate your energy on your hands and say a prayer for your spiritual awareness. Place the candle firmly in front of the candlestick, and place the whole thing in front of the bowl of water. You shouldn't light the candle yet.

Add other objects according to the loas you wish to honor. For example, a shrine dedicated to ancestors will include images of deceased ancestors. The altar of Ogoun will have an axe and a red scarf. The shrine of Erzulie Freda will be decorated with flowers and jewelry, and so on.

Offering to the ancestors:

Preparing an altar is the first step in practicing Voodoo, representing reverence for ancestors. Even if you set up the altar, remember that it is a portal that connects the human world to the ancestors and the loas. Show respect for it, keep it immaculate and clean, and visit it often. You will be rewarded with spiritual growth, energy, personal victories, and remarkable coincidences.

Your ancestors offer you protection and will be there to accept your offerings. They provide guidance and protection, fight for you, and convey messages through intuition and dreams. Choose a photo or picture of a deceased relative whose love for you is unquestionable. If you have no memories of a deceased relative, whether blood or adopted, you can choose an image that symbolizes ancestral wisdom and love and give it a name. You can also choose images of ancestors from different ethnicities. The Egyptians, for example, had rituals of worshiping their ancestors, known as Aakhu ("the resplendent ones").

Place these images behind the water bowl on your altar in a frame or on the wall in front of the altar. This wall can be covered with a white cloth and the images can be stuck to it. Arrange the images until you determine their proper arrangement. You can choose to work with one or several images.

Sit before the altar and, if you wish, ring a small bell or shake a ceremonial rattle (asson) to mark the beginning of your meditation. Light a white candle and, if possible, also light coconut or vanilla incense on the altar. Tie a white cloth around your head if you prefer. Focus on the water in the central chalice. Relax and do any magical exercise you are familiar with, such as counting down from ten to zero or working with the chakras. Breathe deeply and calmly. Think about the ancestor who inspired you.

If possible, try to remember and visualize moments spent with your ancestor. Feel the love that connects you. Imagine this love as a ray of light that passes through the water and illuminates the image of your ancestor's image. Call out your ancestor's name out loud and repeatedly. Tell him or her you love him or her and that you want to work together with him or her. In voodoo, it is essential that the living and the ancestors collaborate and help one another.

When you feel the presence of your ancestors, pour some water on the ground three times to salute them. Do this meditation often until it becomes automatic. After a week or two of consistent and effective practice, prepare a feast for your ancestors.

The meal ought to include the most beloved foods of your ancestors, except for savory dishes. For offerings to generic ancestors, such as those you did not meet in life, include grilled corn, grilled peanuts, fresh coconut, and white foods such as rice pudding, milk, and cakes made from flour dough.

You should place each type of food in a bowl and place a white candle between them. The liquid offerings can be placed into glasses. Pass each plate or bowl over your forehead, heart and genital area and then smell the food deeply (almost touching your nose).

Speak to your ancestors, reminding them that they once were among the living and that one day you will be among them. Ask them to ward off evils such as poverty, illness, unemployment, fatigue, discord, and sadness. Ask them to bring you all that is positive, including love, prosperity, employment, health, joy, friendship, and laughing.

Light the candles and arrange the food on the altar. Then leave the area. After the candles have burned, preferably the next day, dispose of the food near a large tree. If this is not possible, place the food outdoors where stray animals can eat it. Wash the plates, bowls and cups and rub salt on them. Put them away. Do not use them for other purposes, not even for regular meals; reserve them exclusively for voodoo work.

Utensils on the Altar

The utensils are personal and can vary according to your preference. Among them are:

Candles: usually white or colored, depending on the loa. The candle symbolizes the fire element.

Bowl with water: symbolizes purification and life, represents the water element.

Candlesticks: to support the candles.

Bells or rattles "asson": to call the spirits or signal the beginning of the ritual.

Miniature potted plant: represented on the altar, connects the physical and spiritual world.

Image or vevé symbol of the loa: the deity you want to work with.

Offerings: food, rum, tobacco, herbs, breads, fruits.

Incense: to purify the environment, or specific herbs for a purpose. Incense symbolizes the fire element and the air element.

Bowl with sand: symbolizes the earth element.

White towel: It is usually white. But if you work with a specific loa, use the color associated with them.

Human skull (replica), for decoration or for some evil work.

Candles in the shape of a skull.

Mini wooden coffin (to harm).

Bones of animals.

Some utensils may be different depending on the spell to be performed.

The poteau-mitan in the temple is a large pillar that connects the spiritual plane to the physical. It is evident that on an altar, it must be in miniature form. An identical concept is the "Djed pillar" or miniature "obelisk" that is used on the altar in Egyptian magic.

Voodoo dolls

The dolls are effigies (representations of a human person).

There are slight differences between rag dolls and wooden or wax dolls (paket, or wanga paket).

Voodoo dolls made from wood or wax were called "paket" or "pake". Nonetheless, rag dolls did not receive this designation. The term "paket" refers to precisely prepared and dedicated fetishes or amulets (sometimes referred to as "wanga paket"), which usually contain herbs, stones, and other symbolic objects, gathered in small packages. Cloth dolls in voodoo, used for healing, protection or even evil rituals, are more commonly known simply as voodoo dolls, without the use of the term "paket". The term "paket" pertains to a small package containing herbs or personal belongings of the victim, which may be sewn together in the form of a small human figure.

There is a report of a magical ritual with effigies, in which the bokor would pass a rope with a knot over a wax doll, symbolizing his intention, while reciting magical words: Arator, Lepidator, Tempter, Soniator, Ductor, Comestos, Devorator, Seductor.

Driven by the power of his hatred, the sorcerer controlled the victim's fluidic energies. In a fury, he would stab the doll with a dagger and throw it into the fire. At that precise moment, the individual who was cursed would experience severe illness or succumb.

In some contexts, the effigy is also called "dagyde" which means "shape" of that person, and is used to curse or dominate (envultamento). Dagyde is also synonymous with a witch who performs these spells. "Envultamento" is an expression that derives from "to envelop" or create a small package with a spell inside, it is a Portuguese term, but in English the expression maybe is "wrapping".

The dolls could be made from a variety of materials, including wood or clay (as was traditionally done by the indigenous people), or from rags, wool, or in the modern New Orleans style, with a stick and rolled-up threads serving as eyes.

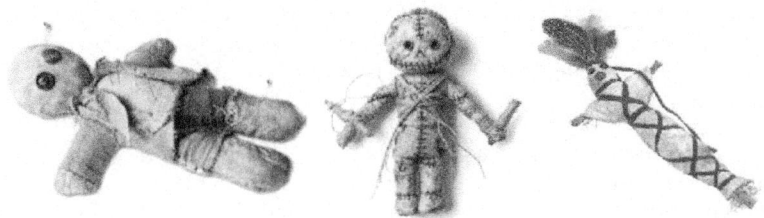

At the end of the book, I share the modern method of making voodoo dolls.

The possession:

Possession is a method of respectful spiritual communication with the loa, which involves the use of specific rhythms and rituals to facilitate the manifestation of spirits, with the aim of obtaining spiritual guidance and protection. During the process, the hougan remains conscious and under suggestion.

Possession is an essential and deeply valued element in voodoo.
As a Haitian proverb says:

> "Christians go to church to talk to God; we go to hounfort to become one with Him."

During the war against France, the bokor performed rituals in which soldiers were possessed by the most powerful warrior loas. Haitian people believed that the French were not fighting mere humans, but demigods. This belief inspired the Haitians to fight with such determination that they were able to free their country.

Rituals and Offerings: Voodoo ceremonies involve offerings, dances, and chants specific to each loa, with the aim of calling and accommodating the presence of the spirits.

Tam-tam rhythms: Possession is often induced by the rhythm of drums (also known as "tam-tam" or "Tanbou kon"), which create an atmosphere conducive to the manifestation of the loas. There is another large drum called an "assôtor".

The atabaques in Kimbanda and the drums in Voodoo play a comparable role in inducing trance states and in the possession of mediums by spirits or loas. Below are some of the similarities between the elements:

Trance Induction Function:

Rhythm and Frequency: Both the atabaques in Kimbanda and the drums in voodoo produce repetitive and continuous rhythms. These rhythms have a hypnotic quality that helps to change the state of consciousness of participants and mediums and induce trance.

Spiritual Connection: The sound of the atabaques and drums acts as a channel of communication with the spiritual world. During rituals, rhythms are used to invoke the loas and establish a deeper connection with them.

Atmosphere Creation: Both types of drums contribute to creating a ritualistic atmosphere favorable to spiritual manifestation. The sound and vibration of the drums define the ritual space, preparing it for the presence of the spirits.

Facilitation of Possession:

Altered State of Consciousness: The intense and continuous rhythm of the drums and atabaques alters the mental state of the mediums, facilitating entry into a trance. This state is essential for the spirits or loas to be able to manifest themselves and temporarily take control of the mediums.

Spiritual Channeling: During the trance induced by drums or atabaques, the mediums become channels through which the spirits or loas can manifest themselves and communicate with the participants in the ceremony.

Energy and Intensity: The sound of drums and atabaques contributes to an intense and vibrant ritual energy, essential to the manifestation and interaction of spirits. The energy generated by the rhythm helps to attract and maintain the presence of the loas.

Rite of Self-Initiation

This small rite, for the solitary practitioner, serves to introduce oneself to the loas, indicating one's availability and being receptive to their energies.

When beginning to work with the loas, it is necessary to establish an initial contact in which we express our desire to dedicate ourselves to their service and collaboration. Once this has been established, we may proceed with the rituals.

1.- Sit facing east in front of a table that serves as an altar. On it, place four candles: red for the east, green for the south (right), blue for the west and yellow for the north (left). Place a glass of pure water in the center of the altar.

2.- Light the candles and repeat the words:

"In the Spirit World there is no Darkness! I want to be a Child of Light! Spirits of the depths of the Waters, Spirits of the Dead, I am here to serve you!"

3.- Touch the water with the fingers of your right hand and wet the center of your forehead, repeating:

"I dedicate my being to the service of the loas."

I ask for your help and I ask you to be present at this altar and in the element that you are closest to, water. I ask you to help me and, in return, I offer myself to serve you. I offer myself to the service of the great King of the Submerged Spirits, Grand Maître Bois d'Ilet."

4.- Close your eyes and notice how the spirits respond. Remain silent for a few moments and then drink a glass of water, as the spiritual power resides there.

Meditate for a few minutes and blow out the candles, clear the altar.

Recipes

Oils, essences, voodoo powders

Essential oils and water are used in Voodoo to consecrate, purify, and energize both the practitioners and the objects of the ritual. They can be utilized in numerous ways. Oils and floral waters may be applied discreetly to the footwear or clothing of the individual being enchanted.

You can buy various essential oils for revenge, hatred, defense, or romantic attraction from an online esoteric store. These oils can be used to anoint voodoo dolls in spells, or to place on the clothes or shoes of a loved one or enemy, among other purposes. Nonetheless, it is advisable to prepare your own oils and incorporate your personal energy and magnetism into the oil.

Uses:

Anointing: Essential oils are used to anoint the body, candles, or sacred objects such as amulets and fetishes to channel specific spiritual energies.

Essential Waters: They can be sprinkled on the altar, in offerings or in the environment for purification and invocation of spiritual protection.

Angel Water (Eau d'Ange).

Angel water is considered to have beneficial properties. It can be used to spray the house or as a spiritual bath.

Items: a dark glass bottle, a portion of orange blossom water, a portion of rose water, half a portion of myrtle water, three quarters of grain alcohol, a portion of distilled water, 1 ml of musk essential oil, 1 ml of amber essential oil.

Mix the ingredients in a dark-colored bottle, tightly sealed, and store them in a cold place.

Five sacred waters.

They are used for cleansing and harmony.

Items: a glass bottle, river water, rain water, ocean water, spring water and holy water.

Mix everything up and bottle it up. The water can be used for bathing, spraying around the house or other areas (work), or for cleaning floors.

Florida Water.

It is used for cleansing and purification (applied around the house or on the target's bedding) and floor washing.

Items: 300 ml rose water, 30 ml tangerine oil, 10 ml lemon oil, 10 ml English lavender oil, 10 drops clove oil, 10 drops cinnamon oil, 10 ml benzoin tincture.

Place the previously conjured ingredients in the bottle and it is ready to use.

Water of Hungary (Eau d'Hongrie).

This spiritual water is used by women seeking empowerment, applying it as a perfume on the body. It can also be sprayed around the house to ward off negative energy, attract good luck, and promote harmony in family matters.

Items: three quarters of a portion of grain alcohol, one portion of distilled water, one portion of rosemary flower, one quarter of a portion of fresh sage, 30 g of Jamaican ginger (crushed in a mortar).

Add all the previously conjured ingredients to the bottle, except the distilled water and Jamaican ginger.

Store the bottle in a dark place for a few days, filter, separating only the liquid, add the distilled water and Jamaican ginger.

Cologne of Love (Cologne D'Amour)

Used to attract love and lust.

Items: a dark glass bottle, 50 ml of grain alcohol, a portion of rose essential oil, a portion of lavender essential oil, a portion of ylang ylang essential oil, and a portion of sandalwood essential oil.

Place the previously consecrated ingredients in the bottle, and it will be ready to use. It can be applied by spraying the area or on clothes (avoid applying directly to the skin).

Attraction Oil

Ingredients: 1 dark glass jar, 1 bottle of base oil (such as almond oil), 1 teaspoon of ground cinnamon, 1 teaspoon of brown sugar, 1 handful of red rose petals, a little rum, 1 thick red candle, 1 chili pepper.

Instructions: prepare the bottle: place the base oil in the dark glass bottle.

Add the Ingredients:

Mix the cinnamon powder and sugar with the almond oil. Add the rose petals and chili pepper to the jar, add a few drops of rum, close the jar tightly and shake it vigorously. Leave the jar exposed to the light of a red candle (thick) for seven days to energize it.

After these days, strain the liquid and remove the petals and chili. Store the remaining filtered oil in a new bottle made of dark glass.

Dove's blood Ink "Dove's blood Ink"

In some spells, it is recommended to write the name of the loved one with "Dove's Blood" ink, which is not real blood. This ink is available in esoteric shops, but you can make it yourself by following the recipe below:

Ingredients: 2 portions of dragon's blood resin (from the dragon tree), 1 small piece of gum arabic, 2 drops of cinnamon essential oil, 2 drops of rose oil, 2 drops of basil oil and 10 ml of cereal alcohol.

Instructions: Grind the resins in a mortar and pestle and soak them in alcohol until they dissolve. Then add the cinnamon essential oil, rose oil, and basil oil, as well as the gum arabic. Filter the mixture and store it in a jar.

Kananga Colony:

Both the Radas and Petro loas are attracted to the Kananga essence. You can use it to sprinkle on your altar, prepare spiritual baths, apply it to candles and amulets, and also as an offering to your ancestors.

Items: a dark glass bottle, 50 ml of grain alcohol, a portion of ylang ylang essential oil (Cananga odorata), a portion of tangerine essential oil (Citrus reticulata), a portion of rose essential oil, a portion of orange blossom essential oil.

Place the previously conjured ingredients into the bottle and it is ready to use. Spray on the ancestor's altar.

The name of this essence is "Kananga" inspired by the scientific name of Ylang Ylang (Cananga odorata). Kananga is also the capital of the province of Central Kasai in the Republic of Congo.

Spiritual Water (Eau Spiritueuse d'Anis)

Used in rituals to work with ancestors, a crystal cup should be placed on the altar of the practitioner who will perform the scrying (divination).

Items: a dark glass bottle, 450 g of angelica seeds, 100 g of fennel seeds and 50 ml of brandy.

Crush the previously conjured grains with a pestle, place the items in the bottle and top up with the brandy, leaving to rest. Stir the solution daily, gently, for a period of seven days. At the end of this period, strain the contents, separating only the liquid, and return it to the bottle.

Eau Spiritueuse d'Anis can be used in scrying rituals (divination through visions) in a symbolic and practical way, to invoke the wisdom of your ancestors.

Space preparation: Place the Eau Spiritueuse d'Anis in a bowl or container, positioning it in the center of the altar. Light candles around it, creating an environment conducive to meditation and contact with the spiritual plane.

Consecration of the bowl: Before beginning the ritual, consecrate the bowl through prayers or chants, invoking the presence of ancestral spirits and protective loas. Offer rum, tobacco, or other items that the spirits like to please them to strengthen the spiritual connection.

Scrying: Gaze deeply into the liquid in the bowl, allowing yourself to enter a meditative state. Eau d'Anise, with its aromatic and purifying properties, can help you open your spiritual senses. As you relax and focus, visions or messages from your ancestors may manifest in the reflection of the water. To intensify the practice and create a darker, more visual surface, place a black cloth beneath the bowl.

Invocation of the Ancestors: While staring at the liquid in the bowl, invoke the spirits of your ancestors, asking them for guidance, protection or answers.

Eau'd Basil

Used to purify and bring peace.

Items: a dark glass bottle, 50 ml of grain alcohol, a portion of basil essential oil, a portion of eucalyptus oil, a portion of chamomile oil.

Put the previously conjured ingredients into the bottle and it is ready to use. Spray around the house, work or any other place.

Four Thieves Vinegar

Used to remove people from the way or cause family feuds.

Items: a dark glass bottle, a bottle of white vinegar, 30 g of rosemary, 30 g of lavender, 30 g of camphor powder, 30 g of sage, 30 g of mugwort, 30 g of mint, 30 g of lemon balm, 30 g of rue.

Mix all the previously consecrated ingredients into a glass bottle and allow it to sit in a dark place for six weeks. After this period, filter the liquid, separating it from the solids, and put it back in the bottle. Then, pour the liquid on the doorknob of the target (enemy) and discreetly move away.

You can also do the following: mix coarse salt in a bowl with a little "Vinegar of the Four Thieves" and let it dry for a few days. After drying, use the remaining salt and spread it over the footprints left by the enemy on the sand of the street.

Third option: Write the enemy's name on a piece of paper, put it in a small bottle of Four Thieves Vinegar, and throw the bottle in a river.

Potion to Curse an Enemy

Ingredients: 500 ml of mineral water, petals of a red carnation, a pinch of lavender flowers, a pinch of black pepper, a pinch of artemisia leaves (wormwood), a pinch of saffron, a pinch of scrapings of a human bone (obtain from a cemetery), a teaspoon of angelica root, a teaspoon of lemon leaves, a teaspoon of black mustard seeds, a dried lemon peel, 1 black candle, 1 dark glass bottle.

Instructions: Perform the ritual on a Monday, at any time of the day. Boil all the ingredients in water for 15 minutes and then let them cool to room temperature. Strain the mixture and transfer it to a glass jar. Place the jar over the Baron Samedi Vevè and light a black candle. Let the candle burn completely.

This potion can be used on your enemy's door, shoes, clothes, drink, or other personal items.

Mars water

Used to fight enemies.

Items: a dark glass bottle, nail clippings or strands of hair from your enemy (or bits of clothing, or a ring, etc.). Water from a swamp, "vegetable tar" oil.

Wood tar is extracted by burning charcoal, using different methods, from the simplest to the most complex distillation systems. During burning, the smoke generated is collected and, from this smoke, wood tar is distilled. Alternatively, "Jewish bitumen" can be used, which is easily found in drugstores or craft shops.

Place the previously consecrated ingredients in the bottle and let them sit for a few weeks, opening the bottle daily to facilitate the oxidation process. The resulting liquid can be poured on the door of the enemy's house.

Other common oils that can be used:

Cinnamon essential oil: To attract luck and fortune, anoint a yellow candle with this oil and light it. Cinnamon is also powerful in love spells, enhancing the energy of these rituals.

Camphor Oil (Cinnamomum camphora): enhances the effect of a candle, drip a few drops on the candle flame. It can also be used to purify your space.

Clove essential oil: To attract luck in gambling, apply a few drops of the oil to your hands or a lucky charm. You can also anoint a green candle with the oil and light it.

Citronella oil (cymbopogon winterianus): powerful to bewitch someone, place it at the door of the enemy's house.

Civet essential oil (Civettictis civetta) or musk: use as a perfume, or in love spells.

Coriander oil: To increase your power of attraction, anoint a red candle with this oil and light it, especially when your loved one is nearby.

Geranium oil (Pelargonium hortorum): attracts good luck, rub in hands. Use in meditation rituals for emotional balance.

Lao Ginger Oil (Alpinia officinarum): rub on the soles of your shoes, it helps you win lawsuits.

Black Henbane Oil (Hyoscyamus niger l.): good for casting curses, anoint a black candle with this oil.

Heliotrope Oil (Heliotropium l.): enhances the effect of any ritual, burn as incense, anoint a candle or an incense stick with the oil.

Hellebore Oil (Helleborus): used to overcome curses, place a few drops on your forehead or hands and recite Psalm 23.

Recipe for Papa Legba Salt, to Cut Down on Harm

Ingredients: 200 g sea salt, 100 g dried rue, 100 g dried rosemary, 100 g dried basil, 100 g nutmeg, mortar, 1 black and red candle (bicolor).

Instructions: Do it on a Monday, Papa Legba day.

In a mortar, grind the herbs into a powder with salt.

After mixing the ingredients well, prepare a hole in the street for the offerings to Legba and place a small pot of black salt inside. Say a prayer asking Legba to open your paths. Light a candle in the place and, when it has burned out completely, collect the salt and save it.

It can be applied to yourself or others. Apply it gently between your eyebrows, at the base of your neck, on top of your head, and a little on your back.

Voodoo Powders

Here's how to make Voodoo powder.

These powders can be applied to a photograph of a person, applied to their shoulder, or applied to their footprints to induce enchantment. Some of the more well-known names are "Hot Foot Powder" and "Goofer Dust".

You can use a spoon to collect some of the sand from the footprint. Another way is to scrape the sand off someone's shoe sole. This practice is known as "foot-track magick."

Many of these powders include several ingredients, including magnetic sand.

Magnetic sand:

You can use iron filings and scrape them between two magnets to generate more magnetic powder, or use a refrigerator magnet (usually malleable) and scrape it on a grater. Shaved azurite can also be added to the mix. A metalworking shop is a suitable location to obtain scrap metal filings.

Goofer Dust Recipe.

To curse the enemy.

The word "Goofer" is thought to mean "bewitched" and may come from the Kilongo word "Kufwa," which means "to die."

Handle the ingredients with gloves to avoid direct contact with negative energy. Mix together some graveyard soil, black salt, sulfur, dried snake skin, and magnetic sand. In a mortar, crush the ingredients well, reducing them to powder.

On a Wednesday during the waning moon, add black pepper and dried insects ground into powder. Conserve this mixture in a glass jar. You can place it over an enemy's footprint or mix some sand from their footprint (or shoe) with the powder. Another alternative is to apply the mixture to the threshold of the individual's house.

Hot Foot Powder.

Mix chili powder, red and black pepper powder, and sulfur. On a Friday during the waning moon, light a black candle and focus on your intention as you ritualize the powder. Keep the mixture in a dark glass jar, but store it outside your home.

Dust keeps enemies away.

Mix graveyard soil with crossroads soil, sulfur, coarse salt, and black pepper. On a Monday with a waning moon, grind everything in a mortar until you get a fine powder. Always handle with gloves to avoid direct contact. Store the mixture in a glass jar and keep it outside the house.

Black salt, also known as witches' salt, can be purchased ready-made in esoteric stores. However, if you prefer, you can prepare it at home. There are several recipes for black salt, but they all include dark elements, ash and burned herbs.

You can make black salt by mixing coarse salt with ash, charcoal, burnt rue and bay leaves, as well as black pepper. Grind everything in a mortar until it is fine.

If you want a stronger black salt, add dirt from the graveyard. You can even customize it with names like "Son of a Bitch Powder" or "Enemy Destroyer Powder", depending on your intent.

Kafou Powder (Carrefour) to close paths

Ingredients: 100 g of cornstarch or neutral talcum powder, 50 g of sulfur, 10 g of cayenne pepper, 10 g of crushed charcoal powder, 50 g of coarse salt, 20 g of ground black pepper, a mortar.

Instructions:

On a Monday, draw the Kafou vevê and place some offerings to this loa on it (rum, a black candle, food, etc. In front of the vevê, take a mortar and grind the ingredients into powder. Light the candle. Store the powder in a glass jar, and place some of the vevê powder inside the jar.

This powder can be thrown into the victim's shoes, rubbed onto their clothes, or placed in a place where the person will pass by. This powder will disturb the enemy's peace.

Dragon Breath Powder (dragon souffle):

Powerful powder for removing curses, casting curses, and for love spells.

Ingredients: black salt, sulfur powder, red pepper (dry), cayenne pepper (dry), powdered charcoal, dragon's blood resin (dragon tree).

Mix the ingredients: Put equal parts of black salt, sulfur, and peppercorns in a mortar. Add a pinch of charcoal and a teaspoon of dragon resin. Grind everything together until it becomes a fine powder.

Place this powder in a small glass bottle.

Note: Black salt can be made by mixing coarse salt with ash or powdered charcoal, and dried herbs like rue.

This powder, known as "Dragon's Breath", will be useful in a variety of spells (see the chapter on spells).

"Phantom Smoke Powder"

When this powder is burned, it makes a lot of white smoke, like a ghost, so it is called "Phantom Smoke." It is used in mediumistic communication rituals or for psychic defense. In the spells section, I added a ritual that uses this powder.

Ingredients: fine salt, sulfur powder, dried white sage (salvia alpiana), myrrh resin (commiphora myrrha), charcoal powder. Note that myrrh is not the common herb, but the resin of the commiphora myrrha tree.

Most often, what will produce white smoke is white sage, myrrh resin, and sulfur.

Instructions:

Mix two equal parts of salt and sulfur in a mortar. Add a tablespoon of dried sage and a tablespoon of myrrh resin. Add a bit of powdered charcoal, not much. Combine everything and grind until it is reduced to a fine powder.

Spells

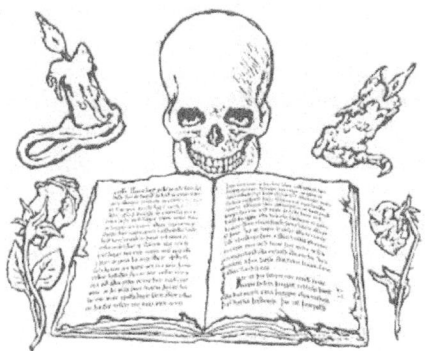

Open Paths or Cut a Curse

Items: "Dragon's Breath" powder (recipe in this book), a thick white candle.

Instructions: Face south, light the candle and sprinkle some Dragon's Breath Powder on the flame.

Ask Damballa for protection, to help solve your problem or curse.

Repeat the process, turning north, then east and finally west.

Finally say:

"Damballa protects me. As this flame burns, so my problems disappear."

If the situation is related to an opponent, you can write the person's name on a piece of paper and place Dragon Breath Powder on the paper.

Lightning Stone for Protection

In Haitian Vodou, "pierres tonnerre" (thunder stones) are sacred and powerful objects. They are connected with thunder-related loas like the loa Ogoun. These stones, often of meteoric origin or formed in special circumstances during storms, are believed to carry an intense spiritual force, derived from the lightning or thunder that creates or energizes them. They are used in rituals for protection, strengthening and invocations, especially in defensive magic practices and to ward off negative forces. Seen as a channel of divine energy, pierres tonnerre are often placed on altars and consecrated with prayers and offerings, strengthening the connection with the spirit world and its protectors.

Items: a pierre tonnerre (lightning stone), aqua florida or Eau Spiritueuse d'Anis (recipes included in this book), a white or red candle, a clay dish, protective herbs such as rue or basil, rum or other alcoholic beverage (for libations), eggshell powder (cascarilla powder) and a white or red cloth (to wrap the stone). Optionally, for cascarilla powder, you can buy a "pemba" in esoteric shops.

Stone purification:

Pour florentine water or Eau Spiritueuse d'Anis over the stone to purify it and remove any residual energy. While doing so, recite a prayer of invocation, asking for protection and power from the loa Ogoun or another spirit associated with thunder, so that he may bless the amulet and charge it with his spiritual strength.

Energize the stone:

Light the white or red candle next to the stone, representing the light and power of thunder. Arrange the protective herbs around the stone on the plate, then serve some rum as an offering to the loas.

Pass the stone through the candle flame and the herbs, asking that it be magnetized with the spiritual energy necessary for protection.

Recite a chant or prayer dedicated to the loa Ogoun or the spirit you wish to invoke, asking for protection from enemies or negative energies. Ask the stone to be a powerful spiritual shield.

> "Ogoun, great warrior, lord of iron and fire,
> Protect me with your sword and shield,
> Guide my steps with strength and courage, Keep away from me all evil or enemy,
> May your flame envelop me, may your light protect me.
>
> Ogoun Feray, defender of the righteous, Be by my side in every battle.
>
> Ayibobo! (so be it)!"

Conclusion:

Sprinkle the stone with pemba powder to seal the ritual with an additional layer of protection. Wrap the thunderstone in the white or red cloth to keep it safe. Carry the stone with you in your pocket, in a small pouch (gris gris), or place it on your home altar, where it will act as a protective amulet.

If you want and are able to chant in Haitian Creole, for greater mantric vibration, here is the prayer to Ogoun:

> "Ogou, gran gèrye, chèf fè ak dife, Pwoteje mwen ak epe ou ak boukliye ou, Gide pa mwen ak fòs ak kouraj, Wete tout move bagay ak lènmi nan chemen mwen,
>
> Kite flanm or anvlope mwen, kite limyè or pwoteje mwen.
>
> Ogou Feray, defansè moun ki jis, Kanpe bò kote mwen nan tout batay.
>
> Ayibobo!"

Prayer to Damballa for Protection:

> "Damballa, ou sekrè, ou gran serpent, Mwen mande ou pou pwoteje m' Kont tout fòs ki mal, Kouvri m' ak fòs ou ak sajès ou.
>
> Fè ke limyè ou klere sou mwen, Ak proteksyon ou toujou avèk mwen.
>
> Ayibobo!"

"Damballa, O sacred, O great serpent,
I ask you to protect me
Against all the forces of evil,
Surround me with your power and wisdom.

May your light shine upon me,
And may your protection always be with me.

So be it!"

Geting Rid of Bad Luck

At dusk, twilight, with a waning moon.

On a piece of paper, write the following prayer in "Dove's Blood" ink (recipe in this book):

"I (name), offer you, mysterious spirits, who guide my life, this prayer. I ask for your help, give me peace of mind and harmony, remove any curse, while this smoke reaches your kingdom. Amen."

Read the prayer aloud.

Place the "Phantom Smoke" powder (recipe in this book) on the paper. Then burn both, allowing a large amount of white smoke to be produced. Wait for the ashes to cool before burying them. If you wish to reinforce the effect, you can repeat the ritual for three consecutive nights.

Influence of Dreams with Gris-Gris

Influence a specific person's dreams.

Items: a small red cloth sachet (gris-gris), specific herbs (like sage for clarity, lavender for peaceful dreams, or rue for protection), a piece of paper with the person's name and intention written on it, a red thread.

Preparation: Place the herbs inside the cloth sachet, along with the paper on which you have written the person's name and intention. On the paper, you should specify your request, detailing the type of dream you want the person to have or the message you want to convey.

Tie the sachet with the string and visualize the person while you do the spell. Say:

"May this gris-gris go to [person's name] and bring [specific intention] into his or her dreams." Damballa, great serpent, may [person's name] receive [the intention] into his or her dreams tonight."

Put the "gris gris" bag somewhere that people won't notice, like near the front door or near the room where they usually spend time.

Finally, thank Damballa. Offer a glass of water, fruit such as apples or pears, or coconut balls, for example. Boiled eggs are also a good offering, as they symbolically represent the serpent's egg. Although serpent eggs are difficult to obtain, the common egg, even from a chicken, carries this symbolism. In addition, the egg is a universal symbol of creation, referring to the concept of the great cosmic egg.

Voodoo binding with Erzulie Freda:

Items: White cloth doll (made by yourself with a piece of a shirt or underwear belonging to your loved one. If this is not possible, you can use a doll purchased from an esoteric store, which should be previously submerged in water with coarse salt and then dried in the shade, to neutralize any pre-existing energetic memories). A pink ribbon as tall as you are. Hair, nail clippings or any other personal item belonging to your loved one.

Stuffing the doll: Dieffenbachia Seguine leaves, pink rose petals, male or female rue (depending on the sex of the loved one), carrapicho/carrapateira herb, and fennel. All dried, can be ground.

A 3x4 photo of your loved one (to glue to the doll's head; optional). Erzulie Freda's scalloped stitch (vevê), voodoo goddess of love (print or trace with pink pemba). Pink-headed needle, 3 pink candles, 3 light blue candles and 3 gold candles.

Fill the doll with herbs and biological material from your loved one. Glue a photo of the person on the doll. Dip your index finger into holy water and baptize the doll as follows:

"In the name of God the Father (make a cross on your head), in the name of the Son (cross on your chest) and in the name of the Holy Spirit (cross on the right and left of the doll), I baptize you (name of your loved one). You are not a doll, you are the living spirit, body, soul, five senses, living nature and brain of (name). So be it."

Stick the needle into the heart area, saying:

"Only to me, (your name), will you dedicate your love, affection and fidelity, in this life, from now on."

Wrap the doll with the ribbon, from head to toe, saying:

"(So-and-so), from now on you are bound to me, in this life, by the power of Erzulie."

Finish the ritual by tying 3 knots in the pink ribbon while making your request. Place the doll on Erzulie's veve (if it is not traced, you can print it and place it on a pink cloth), with the candles lit at the head of the bed, positioning the pink candle in the center.

To please Erzulie even more, spray rose essence in the room and place a glass of champagne next to the doll as an offering. Reaffirm your requests daily. When the candles are extinguished, keep the doll well hidden in your room.

Preparing a basic altar.

Set up a small wooden table, covered with a white tablecloth. Place a glass of water on the table. In a glass bowl, mix some earth with coarse salt. Light a white candle next to it. Add some crystal stones to the altar. Some people choose to place photos of their ancestors or fresh flowers. You can also place the symbol (vevê) of a loa, such as Damballa. Use a light green or white cloth on the altar to harmonize the energies.

The symbol of Damballa is as follows:

On the altar, you can offer a glass of rum, light cigarettes, place boiled eggs, flowers, and coconut. Use white candles to complement the offering.

The cosmic serpent Damballa, or Damballah, is a figure of great power. In traditions that regard him as the creator, it is believed that he formed the universe using his 7,000 coils to create the stars and planets in the sky, as well as to shape the hills and valleys of the Earth. My book, "Obscure Dimensions and Magickal Systems", provides this information.

Greeting:

Me roi e 'Damballah Ouedo, ou ce gran moun, ho, ho, ho, me roi e'. Damballah Ouedo ou ce 'gran moun la k'Ile ou.

(My king is Damballah Ouedo. You are Great, ho, ho, ho, my king is.)

Asking the loas for a favor

In each corner of the altar place a candle:

To the north a yellow candle, to the west a blue candle, to the south a green candle, to the east a red candle.

Place a black candle in the center of the altar. Between the black and blue candles, place a glass of water. Near the red candle, place a piece of paper with your request.

Light the yellow candle and say:

"Holy spirit of the northern illuminated cross, come!"

Light the blue candle saying:

"Holy spirit of the illuminated cross west, come!"

Light the green candle and say:

"Holy Spirit, the illuminated cross of the south, come!"

Light the red candle and say:

"Holy Spirit of the enlightened cross, come!"

Light the black candle, finally, and say:

"Holy spirits of voodoo, listen to me, come to me."

With your right hand touch the glass of water and say:

"Medium of the sacred spirits, waters above and below, worlds of the spirits of the dead and the oceans, I am here to serve you."

Look at the paper with your request and say:

"O light, there is no darkness! We are in the presence of eternal light."

Say the following prayer:

"Powerful spirits of voodoo, what I wish to receive from you is written on this paper. I ask you to help me obtain what I desire so much. I know you can help me, here is my offering."

Rub your palms together and then channel the energy towards the altar. Drink the glass of water, which is now charged with the energy of the spirits. Extinguish the candles and remove them from the altar in the following order: black, red, green, blue, and finally yellow.

Clap your hands and say:

"It is done! Holy spirits."

Keep the candles stored. You can keep the paper with the request in a drawer and read it every day to rekindle your desire. Repeat the ritual whenever you wish.

Another ritual to ask for help.

Perform the ritual at dawn, while watching the sunrise, after taking a cold shower. Light incense and a blue candle, and invoke Legba, asking for help.

*"I beg Legba to come and help me in this work. I want to know the spiritual secrets. I am Luage, your twin brother here on earth.
I beg you, Lord of knowledge, offer me your help."*

Take a moment to reflect.

If you wish for Legba's energies to flow through you, as a medium, say:

*"I wish to be useful, to be your horse, Mr. Legba.
Use me as a focus for your energy to direct to those in need."*

Voodoo curse.

To devastate an enemy.

Ingredients: 6 black candles, musk incense, your opponent's hair, photo of that person, vinegar, black glass cup (or painted with acrylic paint), a black towel.

Instructions: For this revenge ritual, use a black cloth on the altar instead of the traditional white one. Light the incense and black candles. Place the glass of vinegar on the altar. Then say:

"I conjure and invoke the loas of destruction."

Look at the photo and direct your hatred at it. Put the photo in the glass of vinegar. Imagine the person suffering.

Say:

"Spirits of darkness find (name of enemy), destroy his life."

Take the candles one by one and drip a few drops of wax into the glass, say:

"Find (name) spirits of destruction, fill their mind with pain and suffering."

Place the victim's hair in the cup. Say:

"I conjure you (name of victim), that destruction and pain enter your life, that the spirits of darkness stun your body with their vengeance."

Blow out the candles (you will reuse them the next night).

Leave the altar like this for a week, repeating the ritual each night.

Simple voodoo spell to dominate someone.

Buy a thick white candle (one that will last for seven days) and anoint it with "dominating oil". Sprinkle the candle with salt and camphor powder. Light the candle and let it burn. On the third night, gather the remaining powder from the candle and put it on the path where the person usually walks.

"Domination Oil" Recipe:

In a mortar, mix rose, frankincense, honeysuckle, and vetiver (*Vetiveria zizanoides*) to a fine powder. If you are unable to obtain the herbs, you can use rose, honeysuckle, and frankincense essential oils and mix them together instead.

Voodoo spell to destroy an enemy.

Collect spider webs from around your home and make a small ball of cobwebs. Keep them in a black cloth. Find a dead fly and place it inside the cloth, wrapped in the webs, symbolizing your enemy. On a piece of paper, write the following statement:

> "North, south, east, west, spider webs shall bind him. East, west, north, south, bind his limbs, bind his mouth, seal his eyes and stop his breath, wrap him in the webs of death."

Fold the paper and place it in the black cloth. Make a small sachet (gris gris) with the cloth and sew it tightly closed. Place it under a piece of furniture within your home and allow it to accumulate dust. After a few weeks, remove the small black sachet and burn it near the enemy's house.

Remotely influence someone

To influence or control the minds of others, one can invoke the loas. The ritual involves making a magic square with the name of the person you want to influence and clearly visualizing how they look.

You should create a magic square containing the name of the person you wish to influence, while also visualizing their appearance. The magic square is made as follows:

The peripheral lines are made:

```
J U A N
U     A
A     U
N A U J
```

Placing the written name in front of the four directions: East, South, West and North.

Complete the interior by diagonally crossing the square from the bottom left to the top right with the letter on both sides:

Fill in the remaining spaces with the letter that is on both sides of the slanted line:

Once the square is complete, it must be impregnated with the magical intention you want to induce in the person. This is done with each of the letters:

"I imbue this magic square with the power of my mind!"

After the square is infused, it is placed on the altar with the candles. Instead of a glass of water, a glass of an alcoholic beverage (such as rum, cognac, aromatic wine, etc.) is placed between the blue and black candles. The magic square is placed between the black and red candles. The candles are lit in the usual order, and then each of the words formed in the square should be read, from top to bottom and from left to right.

These words are offered to the spirits when they are pronounced.

Say:

> "Mighty loa spirits! I, your Priest and servant, wish to control the mind of (name). Accept the magic square as an offering of my service!

I take into my being the magical powers of the mighty and invisible spirits, present here and now!"

Drink the drink and feel the strength of the spirits flowing within you. Then, return the cup to the altar and extinguish the candles in the opposite order from the order in which they were lit before. Say:

"Loa Spirits, collect this magic square and the intention of my will in your kingdom!"

When the initiate needs a partner of the opposite sex to share his life and magical work with, he can use this practice to attract the desired person. It is essential to be patient and make a careful choice, not only considering physical appearance, but also other important factors, such as personality and charisma.

The mage will use the method described above to visualize the desired person and then place the diagram under the cup with the drink:

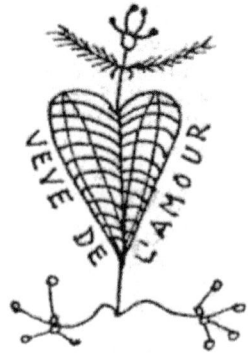

Vevé by Èzili Freda, one of Erzulie's manifestations.

Before drinking the liquid from the cup, say:

"Powerful spirits, give me the powers of attraction necessary for (beloved) to unite with me!"

Voodoo Doll- Spells

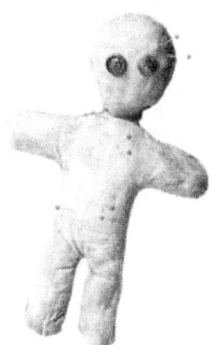

The doll's purpose is to represent the person being bewitched, creating an energetic-spiritual connection with them, whether through personal objects, nail clippings or strands of hair. Traditionally, dolls were made from cloth or clay, as mythologically, it is believed that we all originate from the earth, and clay contains elements common to our bodies. Nowadays, you can use FIMO sculpture clay instead of baking it in the oven. It's a type of modeling clay that is easy to work with and hardens naturally.

The German firm Staedtler Fimo makes this modeling clay, which is sold all over the world. Similar to plasticine and clay, it is composed of polyvinyl chloride particles (PVC). Its main characteristic is that it hardens permanently after a certain period of time. The beige-toned clay, similar to the color of skin, is the most suitable material for the creation of voodoo dolls.

If you don't have the skills to sculpt, you can use molds. These can be found on eBay, Aliexpress or in craft stores.

If you want the doll to resemble the target person, you can even place a photograph of the person on the doll's head. It's important to innovate and do something unique.

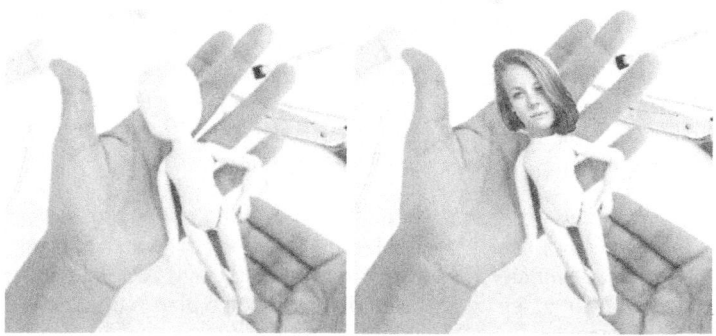

A doll without a photo, or one with a cut and pasted photo. Nowadays, it is easy to get other peoples' photos on social networks.

The "FIMO" clay allows you to insert the victim's personal items (nail clippings, strands of hair, small pieces of clothing, etc.) inside the doll while the clay is still malleable.

I recommend that you always make your own dolls, rather than buying them from an esoteric store. It is essential to go through the creation process step-by-step, involving your personal energy.

Ingredients: Chicken blood for writing, FIMO clay, a paintbrush, 9 pins, some graveyard dirt, nail clippings or strands of hair from the person, a black cloth and a red cloth, black thread, a scalpel, and a photo of the target person.

Instructions: On a Thursday or Friday at midnight, gather your ingredients. If you want to hurt an enemy, mix graveyard dirt and modeling clay. Add mandrake root powder for love spells.

Make a puppet from the clay model, using a mold if necessary. With a scalpel or other sharp object, make a cut in the doll's belly and insert personal items of the person, such as hair, nail clippings, or a small piece of clothing. If it is an enemy whom you wish to cause suffering or illness, add graveyard dirt. Then close the modeling clay. Add a photo of the person to the doll's head.

Remember to also determine the gender of the doll, if it's a female, it should have breasts and a vagina.

Make the following invocation:

> "Jimaguas, Ifá Negre, hear me. Ibo-Lelé, Agouetarroyo, Simby Endeaux Aux, Baron Samedi, power of evil, power of the cemetery, I invoke Damballa, Dambala I pray that my wish be fulfilled. Ogun Negre, may my wish be fulfilled."

Turn the doll over and use a brush and chicken blood to write the name of the person on the doll's back. If the doll is intended for evil, wrap it in black cloth. If it is intended for sexual binding, wrap it in red cloth. Wrap the doll in black thread seven times, tying it well. Then, stick the pins in the area you want to influence.

Please note that if you stick the pins first, you will not be able to wrap the doll properly. So stick them in later. Even if the doll is wrapped in paper, you can still see where the pins will go on its body.

If you place the pins in the head, it is meant to influence the person's mind. If you stick them in the heart, it is to cause pain or a burning desire (make your request as appropriate). In the sexual region, it can be used to cause desire, impotence, diseases, among other effects.

Bury the doll near the victim's house.

Other simpler and faster methods of making dolls.

A clay doll is made to represent the person you want to bewitch.

Inside the clay, place some strands of hair, nail clippings or a piece of clothing from the victim. Then, on a rainy day, place the doll under the roof corner. The water will run off and break the doll. In this way, the person will be influenced by the spell and their health will begin to decline.

Sometimes, instead of clay, tabatinga was used, a clay-like compound made from rare materials found at the bottom of lakes and rivers.

Some black sorcerers even made dolls out of pig skin that looked very realistic.

Another method involves nailing the doll with nails and burying it near the victim's home. The most effective element is either the mage's rage, which creates a mental bond of connection with the victim, or the victim's own belief in the spell (the nocebo effect).

For Burning Love

Prepare a doll and anoint it with honey. Put elements of the loved one inside it. Next, put 9 red candles and 9 chili peppers around the puppet.

Ask the loa of love, usually Erzulie Freda or Erzulie Dantor, for assistance.

To thank Erzulie, offer champagne or rosé wine, anise liqueur, lilies or honey candies.

To get a promotion at work

Create a doll that symbolizes yourself and surround it with 10 green candles and 10 blue candles, alternating the colors. Ask for help from the loa of money, Azaka Medeh, who represents agriculture and abundance, or Ogoun, who, although a warrior, can also be invoked to achieve financial success.

Doll to attract money

This doll will represent you, to attract money into your life.

Items: voodoo doll made with a stick (New Orleans style), green flannel cloth, 3 old pennies, 3 dimes, a bill (from your country), 3 cinnamon sticks, 3 cloves, 3 allspice, 1 whole nutmeg, 1 golden bell, 1 green-headed pin, and 3 candies.

Instructions:

Wrap the green flannel around the voodoo doll. Then, wrap more cloth around the doll and seal the items. Secure the gold bell to the exterior of the doll with a green head pin. Begin to swing the doll with your non-dominant hand (the one you don't write with) for nine minutes.
Repeat the following words:

> "Legba, open the door and clear my path. Bring me money and opportunities to earn money. Remove all obstacles for me.
> In gratitude, I offer you these sweets.
> Thank you, Papa Legba, for your help."

Go to a crossroads and throw three candies into the center as an offering to Legba. The voodoo doll for the money spell should be placed on a table when you return. While at home, keep your purse, wallet, or bag near the doll. Money should enter your life.

Revenge Spell with the Djab:

Objective: use the power of a Djab spirit to attack an enemy, weakening them, causing them spiritual or physical harm.

Items: a black candle, a piece of paper with the enemy's name on it, sulfur powder, a rag doll (representing the enemy), chili powder, strong rum mixed with chili, metal needles or pins, chalk, and an earthen vessel or a "govi".

Use flour or chalk to draw a circle around the altar to define the ritual space. Place the black candle at the center of the altar and place the other ingredients around it.

Write the name of the enemy on the piece of paper and insert it inside the rag doll, saying out loud that the doll now represents the enemy.

Light the black candle and offer rum mixed with pepper to the Djab, asking him to answer your call to punish the enemy. You can recite something like:

"O Djab, fierce and vengeful spirit, hear my call! [Name of enemy] has caused me misfortune, now he will feel your fury. Strike and destroy his life with your relentless power!"

Sprinkle the doll with sulfur and chili pepper, visualizing the enemy suffering. Then take the needles or pins and stick them in the doll, saying:

"With every skewer, I weaken you, [enemy's name]. With every pain, you will feel the strength of the Djab bringing you down. Nothing will save you."

Hold the doll over the candle flame and pour rum mixed with pepper over it while you recite:

"Djab, hear my command! Tear apart [enemy's name]'s defenses, let his life crumble. Nothing will protect him from your wrath!"

After completing the ritual, bury the doll in a place far from your home or in a cemetery, while making the last offering to the Djab:

"The earth takes him, and the Djab destroys."

Blow out the candle and pour the remaining rum onto the ground as a last offering to the Djab. After the ritual, it's important to do a spiritual cleansing to protect yourself from any possible retrogressive energy.

Always offer the Djab something at the end, such as rum or tobacco, to seal the temporary pact and avoid his wrath.

Small sachet to curse someone

Ingredients: a piece of red flannel, Ailanthus altissima plant, 9 pins, hair or nail scrapings of the person to be bewitched, Goofer dust.

Procedure:

Make a small sachet of red flannel and put it in the person's hair. Wrap it around the 9 pins and pieces of the Ailanto plant.

If you don't have any hair or nails, add a piece of clothing, an earring, or something that relates to the person. Also include Goofer Dust (recipe in this book). Next, bury this small gray sachet near the target person's home.

Mini Coffin To Cause Death

Items: Buy a mini coffin from an esoteric shop. Make a voodoo doll of the person you want to curse, as well as 2 black candles and a cursing oil or powder (recipe in this book).

Instructions: Place the voodoo doll that represents the person you want to target inside the mini coffin. If you have any belongings of the person, such as a strand of hair, a piece of clothing, a ring, an earring, or a photo, place them there as well. Light the two black candles, one on each side of the coffin. Then anoint the candles and the coffin with oil.

Now ask the three loas of the dead and cemeteries to help:

"Zo wan-me sobadi sobo kalisso Maître-Carrefour, mwe mem kiriminel.
M'a remesye loa-yo Baron Samedi, l'uvri baye mwe.
Baron Cametière, l'envoi morts".

Which means something like:

I call the way before Maître Carrefour, I thank the loas, especially Baron Samedi, Baron Cimetière, I send you dead.

Afterwards, you should bury the mini coffin in a cemetery. As a gesture of respect, remember to leave an offering for Baron Samedi, including some coins and a glass of rum.

Curiosities:

Many voodoo practitioners are buried in a Catholic ceremony, reflecting the syncretism between voodoo and Catholicism. This may include a mass or other Catholic rituals, such as reading prayers or blessings.

After death, it is common to hold a vigil lasting nine days. This practice is a way to honor and guide the spirit of the deceased on its journey to the afterlife.

The ninth night of the vigil is known as "denye priye", which means "last prayer". This is the culmination of the Catholic ceremonies associated with the funeral. After the "denye priye", the Catholic part of the funeral is concluded, allowing the focus to shift to the actual voodoo rituals, such as preparing the soul for its final resting place and integrating it into the spiritual rituals of the ancestors.

It is widely believed that the remains of deceased individuals, particularly those who played a significant role in the community, such as houngans (priests) and mambos (priestesses), possess significant magical power. Many families and communities take steps to protect their graves due to these risks. This can include building sturdy structures, securing them with padlocks, and even installing security systems around the burial grounds to protect the remains from desecration.

It is common practice in Haitian voodoo to carry the coffin in zigzags or curves through the cemetery before burial. This practice serves to "mislead" the spirit of the deceased, preventing it from finding its way home. This tradition emphasizes the importance of spiritual guidance and protection during the process of death and burial.

When the first man is buried in a new cemetery, the grave is dedicated to Baron Samedi. This practice is intended to honor and ensure the protection of the cemetery as a whole. A sacred cross is erected on the grave, which is not only a Christian symbol but also signifies the presence of Baron Samedi. The intention is for him to become the spiritual guardian of the cemetery, helping to protect the dead and maintain order in the cemetery.

If the first deceased is a woman, the grave is consecrated to Mamman Brigitte.

Possession: In Haitian Vodou, there are several traditional ways of verifying the authenticity of a spirit possession during rituals. These practices are meant to distinguish between a genuine possession and a fake one. One technique involves placing fragmented glass on the floor, which the medium must traverse barefoot. If the medium is truly in a state of trance, they will experience no pain. Another method involves placing chili peppers on the medium's genitals (hougan or mambo) to see if they feel any discomfort.

Nowadays, however, different and more respectful methods are used to verify the authenticity of a possession.

Drawing the veves

The vevês, similar to the magical sigils of Kimbanda, represent the symbolism of the loas and function as "access portals", anchoring the energy of these entities. Although it is possible to draw them on the floor or use a colored printed poster, I recommend the traditional version of drawing them directly on the floor or on a dark board.

For the benevolent loas, Rada, they are usually drawn with chalk (pemba), gravel, or the vevés can be made with corn flour.

For the most rebellious loas, Petro, the vevés are drawn with dark powder (coal or dark ash, sometimes gunpowder and charcoal).

It is important to note that a lwa may have more than one vevé symbol; each lwa may reveal different vevés to the medium (hougan). Furthermore, each vevé may represent a different magical working or aspect of that lwa. For example, Ogoun has a warrior side (Ogoun Feray) and a justice and protector side (Ogoun Badagris). Likewise, Erzulie has the Erzulie Freda facet, associated with love and beauty, and the Erzulie Dantor side, which symbolizes fierce protection.

Vevê of the Ghède spirits

Some believe that crosses are influenced by syncretism and refer to cemeteries. The cross represents a crossroads: the horizontal line represents the material plane and the vertical line represents the spiritual plane.

The two interlocking "V"s evoke the "square and compass" symbol employed by Freemasons, who also have lodges in Haiti. However, in this context, they represent the union of the male and female sexes, symbolizing the birth of the primordial androgynous being.

The three steps or degrees of the cross represent the stages of initiation. The first degree refers to everyday life and is adorned with work tools such as axes and pickaxes, as well as phallic symbols. The second degree evokes the movement created by the asson (sacred rattle) in the air. The third degree, the highest, symbolizes a secret kept only by those initiated into the priesthood, granting its possessor the gift of "double vision."

For the vevê of the Ghède spirits, you can offer: lit black or purple candles, black coffee in a mug, spicy dishes, a glass of rum, and lit cigars.

Veve of Baron Samedi

Similar to the previous vevê, the cross refers to cemeteries and crossed paths, with similar symbolism. On either side of the figure are coffins. The small stars or crosses surrounding the main cross represent spiritual energies, including the loas and other spirits that collaborate with Baron Samedi. The diagonal arrows pointing outwards symbolize Baron Samedi's ability to exert control on both the spiritual and physical planes.

For Baron Samedi's vevê, you can leave offerings like: lit purple or black candles, a glass of rum with a chili pepper, a lit cigar, cooked and spiced meat, and roasted peanuts.

Veve of Ogoun Ferraille or Ogou Feray

Ogoun's more warrior side.

The triangle at the base represents the union of the three great rites: Rada, Petro, and Congo Ibó. This triangle is subdivided into three parts, each marked by "points of tension". The vertical line symbolizes the poteau mitan, the column that connects heaven to earth and the spiritual to the material. At the top, there is a kind of "ceiling" that represents the roof of the Hounfort temples.

In the center of the vertical line (poteau mitan), three loops can be discerned as the horns of a ram, a symbol of fixed thought and authority. Above, a horizontal bar crosses the vertical line, symbolizing the balance the initiate must seek, assisted by the prayer that rises to the sky and descends (the two curved lines). At the top, the voodoo star stands out, representing Ife, the sacred city in Nigeria.

On Ogoun's vevê leave as offerings: lit white or red candles, rice and red beans (cooked), a glass of rum, lit cigars, or corn.

Greeting to Ogou Feray:

"Pou Ogou Feray, mistè kap maché sou planèt Mas.
Mèt foj-la, solda, brave, pwojété nou. Ba-nou pouwa ou.
Aksepté ofran'n nou. Antré nan kè nou, nan bra nou, nan jam'm nou.
Antré vin'n dansé avek nou."

Meaning:

"To Ogou Feray, mystery who walks on Mars.
Master of the forge, warrior, hero, Protect us. Infuse us with your power.
Accept our offerings. Enter our hearts, our arms, our legs.
Enter and dance with us."

Veve of Ogou Badagris

These "grids" may symbolize a fence or several intersecting paths. Some books suggest that it is a spiritual battlefield seen from above. The intersecting lines, which form diamond patterns, and the eight-pointed stars refer to war and power. The lateral spirals are associated with movement and transition, suggesting dynamism in combat. The stars are a symbol of energy and strength, whereas the geometric shapes represent organization and discipline, attributes that are associated with Ogou as a military leader and strategist. At the base of the veve, you can see two crosses, but they actually represent two swords.

At the top of the diamond, the diamond contains three stars, whose interpretation may vary. In my perspective, they represent the three most combative and well-known facets of Ogou, namely Ogou Feray, Ogou Achade, and Ogou Badagris.

You can leave offerings such as a lit red candle, cigars, rum, red beans, mango, pineapple, and yam. Ogou Badagris can be invoked to overcome challenges, face adversaries, or open paths in your life.

Veve of Aizan (or Ayzian)

Ayzian is the loa who presides over initiation, wisdom, and markets. She is herself a mambo. She is believed to be the patroness of hounforts and the spiritual order. Her symbol has two "V's" that are connected and represent the primordial androgyne. The branches end in spirals, which represent the cycles of spiritual growth. The diamond shape, associated with Ayzian, represents the connection between the physical and spiritual worlds, a connection that she facilitates, especially in initiation ceremonies and in rituals to open spiritual paths. The symbol also has some Masonic syncretism. In the central diamond, there is a palm leaf with its well-defined veins. For followers of voodoo, this leaf symbolizes the union of man with nature. During initiation rituals, the palm leaf is used to purify and consecrate the initiates, representing the purity and wisdom transmitted throughout this sacred process.

Offerings such as a glass of water, fruit, sweets, coins, champagne, white or green candles, and coins can be left in the veve.

Veve of Papa Legba

The crossed lines in the veve are obvious and symbolize crossroads, with Legba being the lord of the paths, the guardian between worlds, and of destiny. On the right, Legba's staff is represented. Although they seem rudimentary, the other symbols with a cross in the center are considered to be door locks. However, I also see them as a representation of the four cardinal points or even the alchemical symbol for Earth. At the top and bottom, in a vertical position, are two small leaves, which symbolize initiation and renewal. The curves and spirals in the veve represent the movement and fluid energy of Legba, similar to the spirals with the same symbolism in the risqué points of Kimbanda. The stars and asterisks refer to the loas under his lineage or to the spiritual guides.

At the top and at the base there are two banana leaves:

Banana leaves are believed to bring protection, and offerings to the loas are also left, in some cases, on top of banana leaves.

In some veves, the spirals are considered to be "ram's horns", in the vevês of loas that have more "dominant" or "strong" energy, this is a symbol of strength, authority, overcoming challenges, or even protection.

There are variations of this veve, depending on tradition.

At Papa Legba's veve, one can leave as offerings lit red or black candles, smoked meat, cooked yam, cooked rice, rum, sugar cane, coins, a pipe, and tobacco.

Greeting:

"Pou Legba, gadien pòt Lwa soley. Papa ak patron. Mistè kafou, sous rélasion visib ak envisib. Poto Mitan ki mounté jis nan sièla.
Aksepté ofran'n nou. Antré nan kè nou, nan bra nou, nan jam'm nou.
Antré vin'n dansé avek nou."

"To Legba, the one who guards the door. Solar god, the splendor of creation, father, and patron. Mystery of the crossroads, source of communication between the visible and the invisible, the central pole that extends from the sun to the ground.
Accept our offering. Enter, Lord, into our hearts, our arms, our legs.
Enter and dance with us."

Veve of Erzulie Freda

This is the loa of love. In the center is a segmented heart, with each square and inner point representing a force ready to explode. The voodoo star is at the top, followed by two crescent moons and Legba's staff. This symbolizes that love arises through the union of the masculine and feminine principles, the fusion of water and fire. The large side handles represent the need for balance, showing that no principle should prevail over the other. At the base of the veve are the inverted ram's horns, a symbol of strength.

This veve is often used in rituals and ceremonies to call for love, beauty, lust, and emotional harmony. Both Erzulie Freda and Erzulie Dantor can be invoked to fulfill many of life's pleasures. Their veves are often decorated with hearts, flowers, and delicate symbols, highlighting their respective domains.

On the vevê you can leave offerings such as: lit pink or light blue candles, sweets, champagne, cooked rice, or cigarettes.

Mommy Brigitte

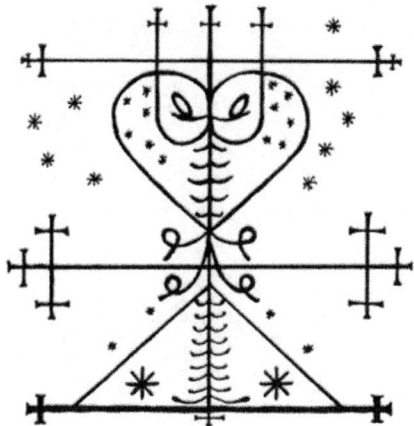

There are several crosses associated with Mamman Brigitte, the loa who rules over cemeteries and the dead, and is the wife of Baron Samedi. She is the wife of Baron Samedi. Through her, souls are given safe passage into the afterlife, while the living are protected from the negative influences of the realm of the dead. Mamman Brigitte rules over the spirits of the dead (ghède) and is often invoked for protection, spiritual guidance, or in cases of serious illness, especially when the cause is believed to be witchcraft. She also protects the graves of recently buried family members.

On Mamman Brigitte's vevê leave: white or purple candles, rum with a chili pepper inside, white lilies, a mug with coffee.

Damballah

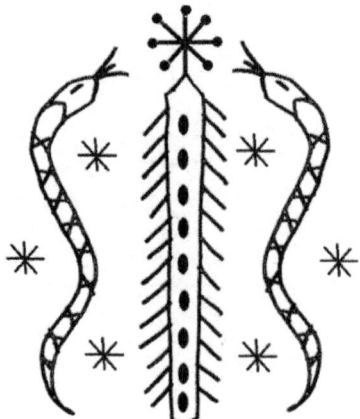

Damballah has several veves. In this particular example, we can observe the two serpents, Damballah Wedo and his female counterpart, Ayida Wedo, who can be understood as a partner or as a feminine aspect of Damballah himself, highlighting the concept of dualism.

At the top is the star of the sacred city of Ife. In the center stands the great mast that connects heaven to earth, known as the poteau-mitan. Damballah is a primordial loa associated with creation and the creator of humanity. He is invoked to bring peace, wisdom, protection and healing.

By invoking Damballa, devotees often ask for assistance, renewal, and help in times of transition.

On the veve of Danballah you can leave offerings: lit white candles, boiled eggs, white flowers, a glass of milk, or honey.

Veve of Carrefour (Kafou)

There may be other variations, it is important to note. In this veve, we can see crossed lines, representing the crossroads, as well as spirals of energy. The circles with a cross inside allude to the alchemical symbol of planet Earth. The intertwined "V's" symbolize the harmony between two polarities (positive and negative) or paths that intersect.

Kafou can be invoked to open paths in one's life as well as block the paths of others. The offerings at the veve include a lit red candle, rum mixed with a little gunpowder, bourbon, a lit cigar, and rice cooked with black beans.

Notice: The design of the vevès is up to you. For the loas of the "Rada" line, it is recommended to utilize chalk or white pemba, white flour, and to draw on the floor, on a board, or on a cloth.

For the "Petro" line of vevès, you can use powdered black charcoal, dark ash, dark pemba, or ash mixed with ground coffee. Some bokor also recommend using powdered brick mixed with ground black pepper. The design can be made on the floor, on a cloth or on a board.

Example of a board or plate:

Tip:

Some people draw the Legba veve on a board, making a "Ouija" board for divination. To do this, they can use a small glass, a ring, or a planchette.

You can draw letters or simply write "Yes" and "No" in the corners. This is an oracle designed to provide short, practical answers.

Glossary

Asson: It is the symbol of the priesthood, a ritual rattle composed of a hollow gourd decorated with stones, or snake vertebrae (representing Damballah-Wedo) and small bones, decorated with beads on the handle. The asson is used to invoke the loas and guide the rituals. When a hougan is formally invested as a priest, he is said to have "received the asson". The rattle is also a clear reference to the sound of serpents.

Bagi: The temple has individual rooms or chambers called "bagi". Each bagi is usually dedicated to a specific loa or group of loas, and is decorated with symbols and elements appropriate to each spirit. These spaces are used to perform rituals and make offerings to the loas, as well as serving as places of meditation and preparation for ceremonies.

Baptême (batèm): A ritual ceremony in which the objects used in the hounfort are baptized or consecrated to the loa (e.g., statuettes, the asson, etc.). Individuals are also baptized.

Baron Samedi: The central figure of the Ghede family is the loa of death, responsible for overseeing the transition between the living and the dead, offering guidance on the afterlife. His symbols include the cross, the coffin, and the penis, with black being his predominant color. During the possession of his devotees, he displays irreverent behaviour: he tells bold jokes, makes provocative gestures, wears sunglasses and a top hat, smokes cigars, eats voraciously and drinks rum seasoned with 21 hot peppers.

Baron has several aspects including Baron Samedi, Baron Cemetiere, Baron la Croix, and Baron Criminel. In all his aspects he is a male loa with a nasal voice, carries a staff or baton, and dresses in black or purple. He is considered the last resort for deaths caused by magic, even if a spell brings someone to the brink of death. If Baron refuses to dig the grave, the person will not die.

Barriè: "Barrie" designates a spiritual entrance or gate that connects the material world to the realm of the loas. It can be represented by specific objects, symbols, or rituals that facilitate the "opening" of this channel between the worlds. This includes the arrangement of certain items on the altar, the performance of specific invocations and the creation of dedicated ritual spaces.

Baton-Legba: The Baton-Legba is a long stick or staff used in rituals to represent and honor the loa Legba, the guardian of the crossroads and spiritual doors. This staff symbolizes Legba's authority and presence, and is often used to invoke his energy and assistance during rituals.

The Baton-Legba is considered a channel for communication with the spirit world, facilitating the opening of pathways and connection with the loas during rituals. Similar to wands from other traditions, such as the Was scepter or the Heka scepter in Egyptian magic, the Baton-Legba is used in voodoo ceremonies to invoke the presence of Legba and establish a connection with the loas. It can be struck on the ground or used to perform specific gestures that aid in the execution of rituals.

Bondyè: Bondyè is the supreme God and creator of the universe, which is equivalent to the God of the Christian tradition. The name "Bondyè" comes from the French expression "Bon Dieu", which means "Good God". He is also sometimes referred to as "Grand Maître", which translates to "Great Master".

Bokor: Houngans who practice black magic are known as bokors, or "those who serve the loas with both hands." These priests serve both the Rada and Petro nation loas. Unlike voodoo priests, who perform rituals in a public and respectable manner, the bokor operates in a discreet manner, keeping his knowledge of potions and poisons a secret, thus avoiding the disapproval of traditional voodoo devotees. The bokor does not have a houmfort (temple) or lead a spiritual society, but he provides his services commercially to anyone willing to pay. The bokor is often associated with Makaya Vodou, and in the context of orthodox voodoo, the term is sometimes used pejoratively to describe practitioners who are considered "witches."

Carrefour (or Kafou): is a loa of great importance, connected to power and transformation, both on the material and spiritual planes. His name, Carrefour, means "crossroads" in French, indicating his crucial role in the intersection of paths, both physical and spiritual. Carrefour is associated with the moon, crossroads, and witchcraft. He's considered the elder brother of Papa Legba.

Cheval: Literally means "horse" and refers to the medium who embodies the loa during rituals. This term is also used in other spiritual traditions, such as Umbanda. The "horse" serves as a vehicle for interaction between the world of the living and the world of spirits, allowing the loa to transmit guidance, healing, and blessings. During the embodiment, the loa can ride on the medium, which is called "Monter la tête."

Clairin (or Kleren): is a type of artisanal rum, usually clear and widely appreciated. It is often used in rituals and offerings to the Ghede loas. This rum is produced through the fermentation of sugar cane or other ingredients, such as honey. It is well known for its purity and characteristic flavor, and is valued both for its quality and for its spiritual importance.

Connaisance (or Konesans): means "knowledge" or "teachings" and refers to the knowledge transmitted orally between the hougans (priests) and mambos (priestesses). This knowledge encompasses spiritual practices, ritual secrets, symbols, and stories associated with the loas. Traditions are passed down from generation to generation orally, thus preserving their authenticity and maintaining a certain level of secrecy.

Débâtement: Refers to the sudden movements or convulsions that occur during the medium's incorporation trance (horse). This stage is marked by an internal struggle, where the medium faces resistance before the loa can take full control. The débâtement usually ceases when the loa completely establishes its dominance over the medium's body, ending the incorporation process.

Dessounin (or Dèsounin): derives from French and means "to dismantle", it is a purification ritual in Haitian voodoo that aims to cleanse the space and participants of negative energies, promoting spiritual and physical renewal.

Desounen: The name is similar, and it is an identical ritual, but i tis intended for funeral rites, where the soul of the deceased is purified and sent to the afterlife, for a smooth transition.

Djab: This term, which comes from the French "diable," means aggressive entities that are similar to the loas of the Petro lineage, but are not necessarily connected to that nation. During the Haitian Revolution, it was believed that the djabs granted slaves immunity from bullets, highlighting their symbolic and spiritual importance. A similar concept can be found in Islamic tradition with the "genies" or the "Djin." Other similar spirits include the báca (or baka), lesser spirits of a negative nature, some of which may be elementals crafted by a bokor sorcerer.

Djévo: During the kanzo ritual, initiates are taken to a chamber inside the hounfort called the "djévo", where they remain in isolation for a week. This room symbolizes a tomb, representing the process in which the initiate "dies" and is "reborn" in voodoo. A similar ritual can be found in Freemasonry, in the "Rite of the Coffin". What occurs inside the djévo is kept secret, but it is in this space that the ritual known as the "laver tête" is performed.

Garde: A "garde" is a talisman or amulet with magical properties, used for spiritual and physical protection. This object may include inscriptions, symbols or other elements that give it ritual power. Gardes can take the form of dolls, amulets, or consecrated items, all intended to protect the individual or space from evil influences. In French, "garde" means "to guard" or "to protect".

Ghede or Guédé: a group of loas composed of many spirits of the dead and separate from the Rada and Petro groups. These loas represent death, sexuality and buffoonery. They are also healers of the sick and protectors of children. Their colors are black and purple, and they often have devotees, when they wear elaborate costumes with large hats, sunglasses and canes, or when they dress in drag. The Fèt Gede (or Fet Gede) is an important celebration in Haitian Vodou dedicated to the Gede (Guédé), which takes place on All Souls' Day (November 1st and 2nd) due to syncretism.

Gris Gris: A gris-gris is an amulet or talisman, often consisting of a small sachet containing herbs, stones, metals or other items with symbolic or magical meaning. It can be used for protection, to attract good luck or to influence events and situations. Gris-gris can be a component of a wanga, prepared and used within a larger ritual to achieve a specific goal. Some fetishes, amulets, gris-gris or dolls can be "charged" with energy by exposure to moonlight (and should be collected before sunrise), by reciting an inverted prayer or by using animal blood.

Govi: These are sacred vessels or containers used to store and protect the spirits of ancestors and other spiritual elements. Govi usually contain symbolic items, such as earth, water, herbs, bones or other elements with spiritual meanings. They are used to invoke and honor the loas.

Sometimes, a consecration of the govi vessel is performed, where the spirit of the ancestor or family member takes up residence, and is then designated as an "esprit" (spirit). These ancestral spirits are venerated and can be consulted or invoked in rituals. The govi is a channel for communication between the material and spiritual worlds, facilitating interaction with the consecrated spirit. This method also protects the part of the humanized soul, called "Ti bon ange", from being transformed into an astral zombie by a sorcerer. It is important to note that the govi vessel holds the essence of "Ti bon ange" and not the spiritual soul "Gros bon ange".

Gros-Bom-Ange: Gros-Bon-Ange (or "Great Good Angel") is one of the parts of the human soul, although it does not represent the whole soul. This concept pertains to the pure and sacred essence of the human being, which maintains a direct connection with the spiritual realm. It can be considered an expression of the "higher self".

Hoholi: Sesame seeds are placed in a coffin to protect the deceased spiritually, symbolizing purity, protection, and connection with spiritual forces that ward off negative influences. However, the exact meaning can vary depending on the specific tradition within voodoo and the type of ritual performed.

Hounfort (houmfor, hunfor): This is the voodoo temple, where the rituals and meetings of the society are held. Each hounfort is led by a hougan or a mambo. The temple must include essential elements for the rituals, such as a square house next to the peristyle that houses the altars of the loas.

Hougan: The male priest is known as a hougan or houngan. He acts as a spiritual leader and intermediary between the loas and humans, and is a respected figure in the community. Like shamans, the hougan can receive guidance and messages from the loas through dreams, intuitions, and visions.

Hounsi: Refers to the initiates, both male and female, who serve the loas. They occupy a position below the hougan or mambo in the hierarchy and assist in the rituals. There are different levels of hounsi, which can progress over time and with experience. After initiation, the hounsi can participate more actively in the rituals, as a member of the choir of singers, for example.

Lambi: A large shell used as a wind instrument in voodoo ceremonies, emitting a deep, low sound. It is especially associated with rituals linked to sea loas, such as Agwè, the spirit of the waters. The sound of the lambi evokes the presence of these spirits and serves as a call to their attention during ceremonies, symbolizing the connection with the aquatic world and its forces.

Legba: Considered the most powerful loa, Legba is the guardian of the portal between the physical and spiritual worlds, where the loas dwell. He also symbolizes the sun. All rituals begin with an invocation to Legba, for without his permission, no other loa can pass between the planes. He is often called "Papa Legba", with "Papa" being a respectful and affectionate way of referring to him, which highlights his role as a wise and fatherly figure. Legba plays a role similar to that of Eshu in Umbanda and Kimbanda, and is always revered first before any ritual involving other orishas. His sacrificial offerings include animal bones and marrow, especially from roosters and goats.

Example of a greeting to Papa Legba at the opening of any ceremony:

"Papa Legba luvri baye pu loa yo, Legba nan baye, Legba nan houn fort mua, Cé ou qui poté drapo, Ce ou Ka paré soley pu loa yo."

"Papa Legba, open the barrier for the loa, You are the one who guards the portal, You alone watch over the loa, Oh standard bearer, and protect them from the heat of the Sun."

Maît-tête (mèt tèt): Meaning "master of the head" it designates the main loa who governs the life of a devotee in Haitian Vodou. This loa serves as a spiritual guardian, guiding and offering protection throughout our existence. Each person has a maître-tête, who plays a crucial role in their spiritual journey, shaping their personality, decisions and destiny. The concept of Maît-tête is analogous to that of the head Orisha in religions of African origin, such as Candomblé and Umbanda.

Mangé Loa: This voodoo ritual involves invoking a specific loa to offer them food, including animal sacrifices, and requesting their presence on earth. Known as "feeding the gods," the "mangé loa" is a ceremony in which offerings are placed on a veve inside the hounfort or at a crossroads when performed outdoors. By feeding the loa, devotees strengthen and energize the spirits, fostering a deeper connection with the invoked deity. Favorite beverages, such as Barbancourt rum or clairin, are poured three times on the ground as a libation.

Marinette: She is a powerful and feared figure, loa Petro, associated with magic, fire, and transformation.

Ogoun: Ogoun is a powerful warrior god, symbolizing strength, power, and masculinity. It is associated with war, fire, lightning, politics, and metallurgy. His color is red, and his symbol is the sword. In the hounfort (temple), he is represented by a continuous flame with an iron rod stuck in its center, and in rituals, by the ku-bha-sah. Sacrifices to Ogoun include red roosters and rum, which are poured on the ground and set on fire. Those who are possessed by Ogoun wear red clothes, carry swords or machetes, and often smoke cigars. This god is equivalent to Ogum in Afro-Brazilian religions.

Pakèt (or Paket): Fetish or amulet consecrated with herbs, stones, and other symbolic objects. This is used in ceremonies to protect or attract energies.

Peristyle: The peristyle is the open or covered space within a voodoo temple (hounfort) where rituals and ceremonies are performed. This central space is dedicated to dancing, chanting and invocations of the loas, and is usually organized around the poteau-mitan, the pillar that symbolizes the connection between the material and spiritual worlds, through which the loas descend.

Servir a Deux Mains: It literally means "serving with both hands" and this term refers to a person who serves both the Rada and Petro loas, while also practicing black magic.

Société: A "société" is a community of practitioners, led by a hougan or mambo, dedicated to the worship and rituals of the loas. Although a société is similar to a coven in terms of ritual and spiritual organization, it is more inclusive, often incorporating community and family ties. This group has a strong focus on preserving traditions and serving the spirits.

Tè: Sacred earth, used in rituals to symbolize a connection with the spiritual and ancestral worlds. Often associated with places of spiritual, ancestral, or religious significance, it can be incorporated into amulets or fetishes to convey its spiritual properties. Graveyard earth, especially when used with negative intentions, can be linked to practices of black magic or dark witchcraft.

Wanga: A wanga is an amulet or fetish that contains ritual elements, such as herbs, bones, and other symbolic items. Wangas can be either beneficial or harmful, depending on the practitioner's intent. The term "wanga" refers more broadly to various magical workings.

Veves: Vevés, are sacred symbols in Haitian Vodou, resembling the scratched points of Kimbanda. Each veve is connected to a specific loa and is drawn on the ground during ceremonies to invoke or honor these spiritual entities. Made from materials such as flour, ash or dust, veves function as portals that connect the spiritual realm to the physical world, facilitating communication and the presence of the loas in rituals. Veves of the spirits of the Rada line (white line) are typically drawn with white flour, while those of the Petro line (black line) use charcoal, gunpowder, or ash. Each veve incorporates symbols associated with the loa it represents: a cross for Legba; a heart for Erzulie, the goddess of love; a serpent for Damballah-Wedo, the patriarchal leader; a coffin for Baron Samedi, the spirit of death; among others.

Zansèt yo: The ancestors. They always accompany the voodooist throughout life, providing inspiration and protection.

Z'etoile (The star): The z'étoile is an abstract entity or concept that represents a person's destiny. It acts as a guiding star, influencing and directing the life path of each individual and determining the events and directions that shape their existence.

Zombie: The term "zombie" derives from the Arawak word "zemi" meaning "spirit". In Voodoo, the process of zombification involves transforming a person into a zombie, usually through black magic and the use of psychotropic substances. This is done by keeping them under mental and physical control, without freedom of will. Although zombies have been widely popularized in films, there are actual cases of zombification. It is believed that a bokor, a voodoo sorcerer, can create astral zombies by manipulating the "Ti bon ange," the soul of a deceased person.

"Fè nwa pou wè klè."

It is in the darkness that the light is seen

Bibliography

Wikipedia

Web Archive

Mortesubita.net

"Black Magick Rituals" – Asamod Ka

"Voodoo Hoodoo Spellbook" by Denise Alvara

"Vodú, Brujería y Folklore en Haiti" -Lucien G. Coachy

"Famous Voodoo Rituals & Spells - A Voodoo Handbook" - H. U Lampe

illuminati-Nehast.com

True Kemetic teachings, Sumerian magic, never-before-seen illuminati rituals.
No Kabbalah bullshit...
Nehast is a Kemetic term meaning spiritual enlightenment.

www.Macumba-school.com

asamod777@gmail.com

https://www.youtube.com/@asamod777

https://www.instagram.com/asamod777/

https://www.tiktok.com/@macumbaschool

www.occult-books.com

http://www.occultbooks.in